YOUR KNOWLEDGE HAS VALUE

- We will publish your bachelor's and master's thesis, essays and papers

- Your own eBook and book - sold worldwide in all relevant shops

- Earn money with each sale

Upload your text at www.GRIN.com and publish for free

Iran Zamani

The Study of Zora Neale Hurston's "Their Eyes Were Watching God" and "Seraph on the Suwanee" in the Light of Hélène Cixous' Theories

GRIN Publishing

Bibliographic information published by the German National Library:

The German National Library lists this publication in the National Bibliography; detailed bibliographic data are available on the Internet at http://dnb.dnb.de .

Imprint:

Copyright © 2012 GRIN Verlag GmbH
Print and binding: Books on Demand GmbH, Norderstedt Germany
ISBN: 978-3-656-94351-8

GRIN - Your knowledge has value

Since its foundation in 1998, GRIN has specialized in publishing academic texts by students, college teachers and other academics as e-book and printed book. The website www.grin.com is an ideal platform for presenting term papers, final papers, scientific essays, dissertations and specialist books.

Visit us on the internet:

http://www.grin.com/

http://www.facebook.com/grincom

http://www.twitter.com/grin_com

ISLAMIC AZAD UNIVERSITY

Central Tehran Branch

Faculty of Foreign Languages -- Department of Postgraduate Studies

Thesis Submitted in Partial Fulfilment of Requirements for

the Degree of Master of Arts in

English Literature

Subject:

The Study of Zora Neale Hurston's *Their Eyes Were Watching God* and
Seraph on the Suwanee In the light of Hélène Cixous's Theories

Iran Zamani Siboni

Fall 2012

I

In the Name of God, the Most

Gracious, the Most

Compassionate

Dedicated to:

My Extremely Concerned Parents;

Alieh and Siavash Zamani Siboni,

And to All The Others Who Are on the Margins.

Special Thanks to:

Dr. Amir Ali Nojoumian,

Dr. Azita Aryan

And

Prof. Jalal Sokhanvar

Table of Contents

Abstract

Zora Neale Hurston is a reputable figure in the fields of African-American literature and Women's studies. The researcher aims at reading her masterpiece *Their Eyes Were Watching God* along with her other fictional work *Seraph on the Suwanee* under the light of the theories of the post-structuralist French feminist critic and thinker, Hélène Cixous. The aim of this study is to scrutinize whether the selected novels could be regarded as examples and models of écriture féminine. The selected novels possess notable features, which led the researcher to study them from Cixous's perspectives. The first leading and prominent feature is the novels' being written by a woman. The second far-reaching feature is the existence of female protagonists within both of the selected texts who revolt against patriarchal figures. By investigating the pivotal notions of openness, multiplicity, body as a means of resistance against patriarchal constructions and the dominance of voice as a subversive element within the texts, the thesis aims to reach this outcome: *Their Eyes Were Watching God* and *Seraph on the Suwanee* are capable to bear post-structuralist as well as feminine qualities. In sum, Zora Neale Hurston, the author of the novels, could be categorized as an example of Cixous's notion of écriture feminine.

Key Terms: écriture féminine, post-structuralist, openness, multiplicity, voice.

Acknowledgement

Above all, I am obliged to confess my indebtedness to God The Almighty who has never deprived me of the eternal support in the process of conducting this research. Special thanks to my dear Thesis Advisor, Dr. Amir Ali Nojoumian without whose supervision, encouragement, patience and beneficial instructions, this research was impossible. I am also indebted to him for providing me with the most essential sources of this research. Thanks to my dear Thesis Reader Dr. Azita Aryan for her knowledge, valuable suggestions and careful revisions as well as the introduction of some useful books to me. I am heartily grateful to her as the main inspiration for the accomplishment of this thesis draws from her literary theory and criticism class where I was first come to get acquainted with Hélène Cixous's ideas. It is my immense pleasure to express my deepest gratitude to the eminent Head of the Department, Prof. Jalal Sokhanvar for his concern, guidance as well as precious information and consideration. Here is an opportunity to reveal my love and admiration toward all of my teachers from the first to the last without whose existence this thesis would have not come into being.

I am absolutely obliged to express my unique appreciations of my very dear parents, Alieh and Siavash, who have undergone an oppressive multitude of difficulties for my education. I am extremely indebted to my husband and my friend, Ayoob; the Tea Cake character of my life, for his understanding and support. I would like to thank Ms. Sheila Bayat for preparing some of the most necessary sources of my research. I am also grateful to my dear parents-in-law for their affectionate consideration, my only brother Mohammad for his magnanimity and my friends, particularly Susan Poursanati for her meritorious help, Hengameh Tossian for her concern and Neda Mirghaffar for her compassion. In the end, I would like to dedicate this thesis to the marginal people including my family and me.

CHAPTER ONE

Introduction

Zora Neale Hurston is a prolific and prizewinning folklorist, anthropologist, novelist and playwright. She is considered as a Harlem Renaissance figure and a New Negro movement's follower. Hurston has written four novels and over fifty essays, plays and short stories, which have been published in different journals, newspapers and magazines.

1. General Background

Hurston was born "under the sign of Capricorn" on January 7, 1891 in Notasulga, Alabama (King 1), notwithstanding she mentioned Eatonville as her birthplace in her own autobiography *Dust Tracks on A Road* (1). Hurston was the fifth child and the second daughter of the preacher and carpenter John Hurston and Lucy Ann Potts Hurston who was a former school teacher. However, it should be noted that in some sources such as *The Cambridge Introduction to Zora Neale Hurston* it is written that she is the sixth child of her family (King 1). She was born just twenty-six years after the end of the Civil War (1861-1865) and the abolishment of slavery (King 14). Hurston's family moved to Eatonville, Florida in 1893 when she was very young (King 1). According to Hurston's autobiography, Eatonville has been "a pure Negro town," which was the first to be established and governed by the Negro community (Hurston, *Dust* 1).

According to King, the young Hurston surpassed in the artistic applications of language quite soon and showed her talent as a storyteller as well as a performer (2). She was encouraged by her mother; Lucy Potts Hurston because education was highly meaningful for her, thus she supported Zora's "creative impulses" (King 2). In addition, Lucy Potts praised

3

her daughter's development of individuality, while Hurston's father was against it. Indeed, John Hurston's first daughter was his favorite and he did not expect having another one (King 2). King writes: "Zora was a female whose natural way of behaving in the world challenged and undermined gender role expectations; in addition she was strong-willed and often at odds with authority." In fact, she had much in common with her father in the matter of her ability to work hard and her desire to search for the horizons (King 2). In 1901, a number of white teachers from the northern states visited Eatonville and the little Zora made an impressive performance to welcome them. The school teachers gave her some books that were highly influential in opening new horizons to her mind toward the world of literature. Some Hurston scholars such as Sharon L. Jones believe that this event might be Hurston's justification to proclaim 1901 as her year of birth (3-4).

After her mother's death on September 18, 1904 Hurston's life underwent a difficult change. As a result of her father's remarriage on February 12, 1905 to Mattie Moge who was only six years older than Zora, she had to be sent away to the Baptist Academy, a boarding school in Jacksonville, Florida. She was successful during her year at Florida Baptist Academy due to her energetic nature and "natural bookishness" (King 3). But they signified her difference as a colored person. One of the most seminal goals of the faculty was to notify their delegates "their proper place" in America, and such leveling was unbearable to Hurston (King 4).

Hurston was faced with a difficult situation as a consequence of her father's negligence in paying the tuition. She lost many of her books because she was deprived of a proper living place and she had to change houses successively. She worked as a servant or sometimes as a babysitter during this time of difficulties. However, she was more interested in the books that existed in the houses of the people for whom she worked rather than in obeying their orders. Once she found Milton's *Paradise Lost*, among some rubbish materials, the account of which later appeared in *Dust Tracks on a Road*: "So I read *Paradise Lost* and luxuriated in Milton's syllables and rhythms without ever having heard that Milton was one of the greatest poets of the world. I read it because I liked it" (98). She was expelled from school at last and after living with her brother and sister-in-law, she got a job as the lead singer's maid in Gilbert and Sullivan troupe (King 4). Her time with Gilbert and Sullivan satisfied her desire to travel. During this time, Hurston's father was selected as Eatonville's mayor for three times. In 1917, he died in Memphis but Hurston did not attend the funeral as she was traveling with Gilbert and Sullivan.

After the trip was finished she decided to attend Morgan Academy in Baltimore, Maryland. Hurston had to claim that she was ten years younger in order to register for free schooling. In other words she had to announce 1901 as her year of birth. She visited May Miller, a Howard University student who encouraged the young Hurston to come to Howard which was traditionally considered to be an institute for the Black's higher education. She graduated from the Morgan Academy in 1918 and moved to Washington to find a job as a waitress and at the same time enrolled in the preparatory courses at Howard University (King 5).

She began her undergraduate studies at Howard University in 1918. At Howard she met highly influential people such as the philosophy professor Alain Locke; the editor of the collection *The New Negro*. Additionally, Hurston entered the Zeta Phi Beta sorority and met Herbert Sheen; her first husband. She played a role in founding the University's newspaper called *Hilltop*. She also became a member of *The Stylus*; Howard's literary club journal where she published her first short story in May 1921. The story's name was "John Redding Goes to Sea" and it was almost autobiographical (King 5). Moreover, Hurston got the chance to take part in Georgia Douglas Johnson's literary sessions and become acquainted with poets, playwrights, novelists and critics who were associated with the Harlem Renaissance and the

5

New Negro Movement. Although Hurston's education in Howard University remained unfinished, she got the chance to come to the attention of Charles S. Johnson, editor of *Opportunity Magazine* (King 5).

Hurston wrote the short story "Drenched in Light" which was more autobiographical than "John Redding Goes to Sea." It appeared in *Opportunity* in December 1924 issue. She won two cash prizes alongside with two virtuous mentions at the *Opportunity* literary contest awards dinner on May 1, 1925 (King 6). She also got the opportunity to meet a number of signal White American intellectuals at the dinner such as Annie Nathan Meyer (1867-1951), an author and one of the founders of Barnard College. Hurston received her associate degree from Howard in 1920 and left the place in 1924 (Jones 4). Hence, Meyer offered her to attend there in the fall of 1925. Furthermore, she met Fannie Hurst (1889-1968) who was a novelist and short-story writer. Hurston became her personal secretary for a short time and almost lived with her for a month. The journalist, photographer, writer, and supporter of the Harlem Renaissance; Carl Van Vechten was the third influential person that she met at the *Opportunity* dinner.

Two months later, Zora's short story, "Magnolia Flower" was published in the *Spokesman* and in September, *The Messenger* published her essay "The Hue and Cry about Howard University". In November, her short story "Spunk" was published in Alain Locke's *The New Negro*. In December she published "Under the Bridge" that shared similar themes with the *"Sweat"* (1926) which had been published in *The X-Ray: The Official Publication of Zeta Phi Beta Sorority*. She joined the publication of a literary journal called *FIRE!!* while she was studying at Barnard and cooperated with young artists such as Hughes and Wallace Thurman. Hurston revised the version of the play "Color Struck," and her short story "Sweat" was published in its sole issue in November 1926. According to King, The Harlem Renaissance can be regarded as a back-drop for Hurston's early works (6). Although Jim Crow segregationist politics were dominant during Hurston's life, the context of most of her works was quite in contrast with "Jim Crow" system of laws that separated African-Americans from white people (King 7).

At Barnard, Hurston was the only black student (King 6). She was the student of Franz Boas (1858-1942), the renowned Columbia University anthropologist. According to King, Hurston began her pioneering research in the South and the Caribbean under his influence and by means of his fellowships. Hurston cooperated with Ruth Benedict and Margaret Mead to conduct some of her researches as well. Hurston got her B.A in anthropology in 1927 at the age of 36 and went to take courses as a graduate student in anthropology at Columbia University for two years (7).

In 1927, Hurston traveled to the south to do a research fellowship arranged by Boas in order to collect folk songs and folk tales. During her travels, and in Alabama, Hurston interviewed Cudjo Lewis; the last survivor of Africans from the last slave ship (King 7). She stopped to give lectures at schools together with Langston Hughes on the way to the south during the summer of 1927. Hurston got informed about a rich patron of arts named Charlotte Osgood Mason (1854-1946). They were introduced to each other on September 20, 1927 and signed a contract in December 1927. Mason promised to support Hurston's writings and research for the following years (King 8).

Hurston continued her literary production by publishing her account of the interview with Cudjo Lewis in addition to another article in the *Journal of Negro History* in October 1927. She published her essay, "How It Feels to Be Colored Me," in *The World Tomorrow* in May 1928. She was satirized as Sweetie Mae Carr in Wallace Thurman's *Infants of the Spring* (1928) which was a satirical novel about the black Harlem scholars. Between 1930 and 1932, she collected material for her book *Mules and Men*. In 1931 and 1933, she published "Hoodoo in America" in the *Journal of American Folklore* and "The Gilded Six-Bits" in *Story*. She contributed six stories to Nancy Cunard's anthology, *Negro*, and published both her first

novel *Jonah's Gourd Vine* and "The Fire and the Cloud" in *Challenge* (King 8).

Hurston had performing abilities and theatrical experiences, as well. Her first formal

theatrical experiences were during the early 1930s. In 1930 she collaborated on the play *Mule*

Bone with Langston Hughes. In 1931 she wrote for *Fast and Furious* theatrical review. In

January 1932, her other theatrical review entitled *The Great Day* was premiered on Broadway

at the John Golden Theatre. She worked on a concert program in Winter Park, Florida and in

1933 she staged in *From Sun to Sun*, a version of *the Great Day* there (King 9).

According to Porter's *Jump at de Sun: The Story of Zora Neale Hurston*, Hurston founded

the school of dramatic arts "based on pure Negro expression" at the Bethune-Cookman in

Daytona Beach in 1934 (66). This action caused her to receive the Bethune-Cookman College

Award for Education and Human Relations in 1956. She went to watch the production of

Signing Steel (another version of *Great Day*) in Chicago (King 9). In 1935, she joined the

Works Progress Administration's Federal Theatre Project to teach drama. She was a drama

instructor at North Carolina College for Negroes at Durham. During this time, she had the

opportunity to meet the famous drama university professor, Paul green. The titles of her plays

that appeared in *The Copyright Drama Deposit Collection* (1977) include "Cold Keener: A

Review", "De Turkey and de Law: A Comedy in Three Acts", "Forty Yards", "Lawing and

Jawing", "Meet the Mamma: A Musical Play in Three Acts", "The Mule-Bone: A Comedy of

Negro Life in Three Acts", "Poker!", "Polk County: A Comedy of Negro Life on a Sawmill

Camp with Authentic Negro Music in Three Acts", "Spunk" and "Woofing" (King 9).

Hurston was extremely busy during the decade of the Great Depression which was the

outcome of 1929 Stock market crash. The negative point of this era was that this period's

female authors "were seriously overshadowed by their male counterparts" (King 29).

Anyhow, Hurston fell in love with a man named Percival Hunter whom she called "the love of her life" (King 10). During 1936 and 1937 she traveled to Haiti and Jamaica to collect folk material. She received Guggenheim Fellowships that supported her travels. She used the collected information to write her book *Tell My Horse* (1938). Hurston wrote her well-known masterpiece, *Their Eyes Were Watching God* (1937) in Haiti just over a seven-week period. Many fictions of the early twentieth century written by African Americans were meant to present their protagonists' longing and quest in the process of becoming a full and intelligent human being. Hurston's *Their Eyes Were Watching God* can be categorized under this group of works. She joined a Federal Writer's Project in Florida to cooperate *The Florida Negro* in 1938. In 1939, Hurston received an honorary Doctor of Letters degree from Morgan State College, published "Now Take Noses" in *Cordially Yours* and her third novel, *Moses, Man of the Mountain* (King 10). According to King, she was so busy during this period that she could not attend her classes and failed to fulfill the requirements for the Ph.D. in anthropology at Columbia. Hurston became the most published black woman writer of this era, however. The only personal incident in this period was her getting married to the much younger Albert Price III, in 1939 in Fernandina, that ended in divorce four years later (10).

Hurston published her autobiography called *Dust Tracks on a Road* in 1942. She had worked on its manuscript since 1941. Her other 1942's publications include "Story in Harlem Slang" in the *American Mercury* and a profile of Lawrence Silas in the *Saturday Evening Post.* "The 'Pet Negro' System" and "My Humiliating Jim Crow Experience" were included in *American Mercury* and *Negro Digest* in 1943. Hurston married again in 1944, this time to a businessman called James Howell Pitts. They divorced eight months later. *Mrs. Doctor* was the name of a novel written during this time which dealt with the upper-class blacks. It was rejected by Hurston's publisher, Bertram Lippincott. She continued to work on shorter writings including: "The Rise of the Begging Joints," "Crazy for Democracy," both in 1945 and wrote a review of Robert Tallant's *Voodoo in New Orleans* in 1948. She published her fourth novel, *Seraph on the Suwanee* in October 1948 (King 10). *Seraph on the Suwanee* was published after the Second World War which was a prosperous time for the United States. This novel depicts an ideal white family in the course of their achievement of the American Dream (King 33). "Waste and Whiteness: Zora Neale Hurston and the Politics of Eugenics" is a significant article written about this novel by Chuck Jackson and printed in *The American Review* in 2000. Jackson believes that Hurston's focus on notions such as "abjection," "waste" and "the construction of class and gender identities" among a group of poor whites who are called "Crackers" throughout the novel, reflect the issue of "eugenics" which was dominant in 1920s (639-660).

According to King, in September 1948, Hurston was "falsely accused of molesting a ten-year-old boy." Although she was released by providing evidence that she was in Honduras at that time and "the case was dismissed six months later," her life underwent a serious damage thereupon and she could never recover from the pain brought up by this outrage (10).

She continued her works by writing for magazines and newspapers for the rest of her life. One of these articles was "Conscience of the Court" which was published in the *Saturday Evening Post*, while working as a maid in Rivo Island, Florida during this time. She published another article in *Saturday Evening Post* in April 1950, as well. It was called "What White Publishers Won't Print." Before moving to Belle Glade in winter, she published "I Saw Negro Votes Peddled" in the *American Legion Magazine*. Hurston's "Why Negro Won't Buy Communism" was published in the *American Legion Magazine* in June 1951 and "A Negro Voter Sizes Up Taft" was published in the *Saturday Evening Post* on December 8, 1951. Hurston was selected by the *Pittsburgh Courier* to work on the Ruby McCollum case in which a black woman murdered her white lover who was a white doctor (King 11).

Hurston tried seriously to work on the life of Herod the Great but was unable to find a publisher for it (King 11). Between 1951 and 1956, she lived a simple modest living in Eau

Gallie, Florida. She became a librarian at Patrick Air Force Base in Florida but was fired in 1957. Between 1957 and 1959, she wrote a column on "Hoodoo and Black Magic" for the *Fort Pierce Chronicle*. She also worked as a substitute teacher at Lincoln Park Academy in Fort Pierce (King 11).

Zora Neale Hurston worked until she could no longer produce. She suffered a stroke in the early 1959. As a result of the stroke she was forced to go to the St. Lucie County Welfare Home. Hurston passed away at the cause of hypertensive heart disease on January 28, 1960 in the most boisterous decade of the twentieth century which was marked by murders, assassinations and revolutions in America and in the rest of the world (King 34). According to King, the receiver of multiple honors and awards and the writer of numerous novels, reviews, plays and articles whose picture appeared on the cover of *Saturday Review* was buried in an unmarked grave at Fort Pierce's cemetery, the Garden of Heavenly Rest (11). Alice Walker searched for her grave but unsuccessful to find its exact location, placed a gravestone on an unmarked grave in the general area that Hurston was buried and marked it as Hurston's grave in August 1973. Walker published "In Search of Zora Neale Hurston" in *MS.*, to revive her name and literary influence (King 12).

Hurston's awards, honors and fellowships include a Rosenwald Foundation Fellowship, two Guggenheim fellowships, one of which was applied to study folklore in the West Indies. An Honorary Doctor of Letters Degree from Morgan State College, an Anisfeld-Wolf Book Award, the Howard University Distinguished Alumni Award and Bethune-Cookman College's Award for Education and Human Relations among others.

Hurston was highly concerned with the folklore rather than "the racialized social oppression" which was a major aspect of American life (King 31). The celebration of everyday lives of black people is extensively illuminating in her works despite the dogmatic socio-economic atmosphere that prevailed her time and life. She was criticized and blamed by

11

many of her male counterparts like W.E.B Du Bios and Richard Wright. She was considered as a conservative, particularly in her later life. King regards her as a "Republican" who was "largely influenced by Enlightenment reasoning" (King 24). Hurston displays her individualism and her basic belief in self-determination. She insisted on individual merit and privileged it over racial enterprise throughout her autobiography in *Dust Tacks on a Road* (215-26). She believed that "radical individualism" would solve America's social problems (King 24). Unlike her Harlem Renaissance colleague; Langston Hughes, she did not favor the Soviet Union. She was a fan of the politician Booker T. Washington. But she cannot be considered to be extremely conservative in the researcher's point of view because she objected to the capitalist and imperialist tendencies of America and other countries. Hurston was intensely against the interventionist policies of Roosevelt and President Harry Truman. When Truman attacked Japan with atomic bombs, Hurston called him "the Butcher of Asia" (*Dust* 259). She evidently writes about imperialist regimes such as England and America in *Dust Tracks On A Road*: "But actually, the British Government does just that in India, to the glory of the democratic way . . . And the very people who claim that it is a noble thing to die for freedom and democracy cry out in horror when they hear tell of a "revolt" in India." She goes on to criticize her own country and its government: "We, too, have our Marines in China. We, too, consider machine gun bullets good laxatives for heathens who get constipated with toxic ideas about a country of their own" (259). Thus, it is taken for granted that though Hurston believes in radical individuality and "individual ability" as the only defense against the social disasters, she did not approve of the interventionist deeds of the imperialist governments at all (251).

Her feelings expressed in chapter fifteen of the same work reveal that she deconstructs religious practice as she deconstructed the idea of racial unity in "My People! My People!" appearing in *Dust Tracks on a Road* (235-46). She was hopeful that her sense of humor would

12

save her from the personal, racial or national haughtiness. Moreover, her literary productions prove that Hurston was against the ideology of proper womanhood that was dominant in nineteenth and twentieth century and as a consequence in the literary productions related to that kind of ideology. The notion of true womanhood places the working class women as the opposite and negative counterpart of bourgeois white women who were characterized by their "domesticity", "piety", "purity", and "submissiveness" (King 24-5).

During the flourishing of black women's literature in the final decades of the twentieth century, Hurston's narratives, especially *Their Eyes Were Watching God* became famous again. The topic of the black female sensuality has been especially explored in this novel. It revealed a history of black female biological objection, moreover this novel influenced on Gwendolyn Brook's *Maud Martha* (1956), Toni Morrison's *The Bluest Eye* (1970) and *Sula* (1974), Alice Walker's *The Color Purple* (1982) and Alice Randall's *The Wind Done Gone* (2001). *I Love Myself When I Am Laughing and Then Again When I Am Looking Mean and Impressive* (1979) is Walker's dedication to Zora Neale Hurston. In this dedicatory work, Walker described Hurston in words and ways that she later used to express her womanist aesthetic. Bringing back Hurston to literary life became a central element in the second and third waves of Black feminist thought. She is known as one of the most notable figures in American literary history and one of the five or six most recognized African American writers in the world and the literary fore-mother of the next generations of female authors (King 12).

1.2. The Argument

This thesis aims at studying Zora Neale Hurston's *Their Eyes Were Watching God* and *Seraph on the Suwanee* in the light of post-structuralist feminist theories of Hélène Cixous, particularly her concept of écriture féminine. In brief, the selected texts are going to be analyzed in order to discover whether they could be regarded as models of writing the body.

The reason that the writer of the thesis seeks to study the text under the light of Cixousian theories is that both of the mentioned novels, are written by the distinguished African-American woman writer Zora Neale Hurston. She is considered as a modernist literary figure. In addition, she has added a great contribution to the Harlem Renaissance. Her *Their Eyes Were Watching God* is considered as her major work and a literary masterpiece. About this novel Alice Walker writes in her "In Search of Zora Neale Hurston" published in *Ms. Magazine*: "There is no book more important to me than this one" ("Zora Neale Hurston"). Although *Seraph on the Suwanee* is regarded as Hurston's failure by many critics, the *Saturday Review of Literature* considers it as "A simple, colorfully written, and moving novel of life among the Florida Crackers" (Cited in "books"). Moreover, the protagonists in both of the novels are women whose experiences construct the currents of the novels. The question that is raised here is that whether these factors are satisfactory enough to call these works as examples of écriture féminine.

In spite of the importance of a work to be written by a woman writer and concentration on women's experiences in all feminist studies, there are other significant elements in a text that should be inspected by means of post-structuralist reading strategies. It can be inspected in Cixous's essay "The Laugh of the Medusa," where she has written:

> It is by writing, from and toward women, and by taking up the challenge of speech which has been governed by the phallus, that women will confirm women in a place other than that which is reserved in and by the symbolic, that is in a place other than silence. (*Signs* vol.1 No.4 881)

She starts her essay by stating that: "I shall speak about women's writing: about *what it will do*" (875). She continues in the third paragraph by writing: "I write this as a woman, toward women" and somewhere later she inscribes: "women are body. More body, hence more writing" (885-6). The addressee in almost all parts of the essay is "woman," and she constantly exploits the pronoun "she". However, Cixous praises the texts that are produced by

14

a number of male writers. To name a few, James Joyce, Franz Kafka, Jean Genet and Heinrich Von Kleist are among the prominent literary figures whose works have been taken into consideration by Cixous. Therefore, it can be assumed that the fact that a literary work is written by a woman is not sufficient to label a work as feminine writing.

The other problem is that Cixous regards poetry as the arena where feminine writing could be flourished as traced in both "The Laugh of the Medusa" and "Sorties." In "The Laugh of the Medusa" she writes: "But only poets – not the novelists, allies of representationalism. Because poetry involves gaining strength through the unconscious and because the unconscious, that other limitless country, is the place where the repressed manage to survive: women, or as Hoffman would say, fairies" (*Signs* vol.1 No.4 881). Thereupon, the other question which is raised is that are the selected novels capable of being studied under the light of Cixous's ideas? The answer would be positive on the condition that the texts bear a number of special traits. These particular features are concentrated on language which according to Cixous is "our unlimited territory which always precedes us" (Sellers xix).

To attain the post-structuralist characteristics within the novels and achieve the desirable goals, some discussion questions should be raised. These discussion questions are going to be worked out throughout the next chapters and fulfilled within the last chapter. The questions that the thesis is faced with would be:

- What is the definition of féminine?
- What is écriture féminine and what are the main characteristics of it?
- How a text should be studied in the light of Cixous's post-structuralist feminist theories? What are the elements that should be put under observation?
- Is there any relationship between desire and feminine writing?
- Are there any references to body? Are the texts concerned with sensuality?
- Does the author reveal feminine libido? Is there any evidence of self-censorship?

- How is the meaning proliferated in the texts?

- Are there any metaphors or other literary figures that produce multiplicity within the texts?

- Is there any lack of repressive structure within the texts?

- How is patriarchy deconstructed in the selected stories?

- Are there any fixed gender roles that are resisted and substituted by new ones?

- Are the silenced women emancipated?

- How does voice help the protagonists to reach emancipation and independence?

The researcher has to ponder on the aforementioned questions to achieve appropriate results in reading Hurston's selected novels under the light of Cixousian methodology, and support the fact that the characteristics of feminine writing can be perceived within them. The answers will also support the argument that Hurston has written by means of what Cixous calls voice.

As it was mentioned previously, the selected novels; *Their Eyes Were Watching God* and *Seraph on the Suwanee* are both written by Hurston, who is a renowned writer not only in the field of women's studies and Afro-American studies but also in the literature of the world. Cixous expresses her dissatisfaction with the male-oriented reading lists that are presented to students in the universities; hence one of the reasons that this research is worth being done is that it introduces a female writer to the academic curricula especially to Iranian academic arenas where both Hurston and Cixous are less acclaimed figures. A work should be begun, as Cixous declares on "the presence of women in literature, on what sexuality signifies what the body signifies in literature" (Cited in Sellers xxvii). This is the mainspring of conducting this research; to remind the presence of women in literature. Hurston has personally tried to display the signification of body in literature, as well. There is a constant existence of femininity, *jouissance* and sensuality. Furthermore, what is most significant in post-

16

structuralist feminist texts is: "a privilege of voice" (Cixous, Clément 92). The selected novels bear a rhythmic language. Moreover, there are other proofs of the existence of voice that will be discussed in chapter four. There are critics who believe that Hurston's works have got the capacity to be read by post-structuralist approaches. Virginia Heffernan is one of those critics. She writes about *Their Eyes Were Watching God* as a work which "New readers found a forceful, erotic, well-wrought story about a black woman by a black woman, and academics in newly formed African-American studies departments had particular need for it. For one reason, its narrative technique, which is heavy on free-indirect discourse, lent [*sic*] itself to poststructuralist analysis" (*New York Times March* 4, 2005). Although *Seraph on the Suwanee* has not received as much reputation as *Their Eyes Were Watching God*, it bears similar post-structuralist qualities. The heroine's final rebellions against her husband via regaining voice and realizing her feminine power are among the novel's anti-patriarchal attitudes.

To sum up, Cixous seeks for a manner of writing that awakens the "exploration of woman's powers: of her power, her potency, her ever-dreaded strength, of the regions of femininity" (Eagleton, *Feminist* 324). The affairs of the heroines in both stories, their states of minds and mentalities, the portraits of their feelings and the illuminating delineations of their emotions, their quest and exploration for potency, the language and rhythm of the texts, the voice and the riot against phallocentrism are convincing elements which support these novels' competency to be studied in a satisfactorily under the light of Cixousian post-structuralist feminism.

1.3 Literature Review

The major sources that this thesis has utilized can be categorized under three groups. The first group of sources is the novels that are selected for the very aim of this thesis. The names of the novels that are the primary sources of this project are *Seraph on the Suwanee* and *Their*

Eyes Were Watching God written by Zora Neale Hurston. Both of the copies of the novels used by the researcher have been published by the Harper Perennial publishing house. *Their Eyes Were Watching God* is going to be addressed as *Their Eyes*, while *Seraph on the Suwanee* is going to be introduced as *Seraph* throughout the thesis.

The second group of books considers the approach and critical theory that is chosen to study the novels. The theoretical sources that this thesis is heavily based on are: the second edition of *Feminist Literary Theory; A reader*, edited by Mary Eagleton and published by Blackwell & Wiley Publishing in 1996, which is a collection of fundamental essays along with relative introductions in the field of feminist literary criticism and Mary Eagleton's *Working with Feminist Criticism* by Blackwell Publishers in 1996, and the third edition of *A Reader's Guide to Contemporary Literary Theory* by Raman Selden and Peter Widdowson, published by Harvester Wheatsheaf and printed in Iran by Daha Publishing in 1381. *Working With Feminist Criticism* is a highly applicable and useful source to introduce feminist theory. It includes tangible introductions to distinct types of feminisms and the techniques by which the researcher can apply them on the selected contexts. Selden and Widdowson's *Reader's Guide* offers historical reports on critical traditions from new criticism, moral formalism and F.R. Leavis to feminist theories. The section of feminist theories commences from first-wave feminist criticism and ends in "Black, women of colour and Lesbian literary theories." Another influential book that assisted the researcher to handle with post-structuralist feminist theory is the second edition of *Sexual/Textual Politics* by Toril Moi published by Routledge in 1985. Moi's book consists of two major approaches to feminist literary theory; the Anglo-American and the French. She discusses the major critics of these trends in detail. The thesis is highly devoted to Hélène Cixous and Catherine Clément's *The Newly Born Woman*. This book has been translated into English by Betsy Wing. This precious book consists of unique essays by Clément and Cixous. The copy that is used by the researcher has been published by

18

the University of Minnesota Press in 1986. Cixous's significant essay, "Sorties: Out and Out: Attacks/Ways Out/Forays" appears in this book. Emancipation from the dichotomies that are deeply rooted in Western Culture is the primary goal of this essay. The concepts of otherness and bisexuality are discussed within this article. The *Routledge Companion to Feminism and Postfeminism*, edited by Sarah Gamble, published by Routledge and copyrighted in 1998 and 2001 is another source book. The Second Edition of *Critical Theory today; A User-Friendly Guide* by Lois Tyson published by Routledge; Taylor & Francis Group in 2006 and the Second edition of *An Introductory Guide to Post-structuralism And Postmodernism* by Madan Sarup which is published by Harvester Wheatsheaf in 1993 are among other source books. The third edition of *The Critical Tradition; Classic Texts and Contemporary Trends* by David H. Richter and published by Bedford/St Martin's and *Signs*, vol. 1, No. 4 (Summer, 1976) are two critical resources in which the copy of Cixous's most famous essay "The Laugh of the Medusa" is available. The thesis owes a lot to "The Laugh of the Medusa" that has been translated by Keith Cohen and Paula Cohen into English in 1976. In this essay, Cixous argues about the liberating effect of women's writing and seeks to emerge the notion of body to text. She impels women to break their silences and enter the site of speaking.

The third group of major sources includes books and articles that are about the selected novels or their author's literary attitudes. The most helpful and widely used books are *Bloom's Modern Critical Views: Zora Neale Hurston – New Edition* edited by Harold Bloom and copyrighted in 2008 by Infobase Publishing and Lovalerie King's *The Cambridge Introduction to Zora Neale Hurston* published by the Cambridge University Press in 2008. Bloom's book is a compilation of remarkable essays on Zora Neale Hurston's works. King's book aims at introducing Hurston and her works in order to prove Hurston's significance to different literal, intellectual and anthropological arenas. It consists of four chapters that are entitled as "Life," "Contexts," "Works," and "Critical Reception." Furthermore, the researcher has taken advantage of Zora Neale Hurston's *Dust Tracks on a Road* that is an autobiography full of creativity and humor. Although there seems to be some false information within the book, it is undoubtedly helpful to learn about Hurston's life and works. The copy in the hands of the researcher has been published in 1996 by HarperCollins. *I Love Myself: When I Am Laughing...and Then Again When I Am Looking Mean and Impressive* is another work that includes a collection of excerpts from Hurston's fictions and novels, essays, short stories, autobiography and an introduction by Mary Helen Washington. It has been edited by Alice Walker later and published by Feminist Press in 1979. Other source books include Tom McGlamery's *Protest and the Body in Melville, Dos Passos, and Hurston*, edited by William E. Cain and published by Routledge and Sharon L. Jones *Critical Companion to Zora Neale Hurston; A Literary Reference to Her Life and Work* by Facts on File in 2009. In terms of articles, this thesis is highly devoted to a thesis with the title "Discourse on Sexuality in the works of Zora Neale Hurston" fulfilled by Jan Beneš in Masaryk University, 2011 and also "Zora Neale Hurston as an Independent Woman: A lonely place in the Harlem Renaissance" accomplished by Timothy Lyle in 2005.

In order to read literary works and doing a project about them, glossaries, dictionaries and encyclopedias perform highly significant roles as well. J.A Cuddon's *The Penguin Dictionary of Literary Terms and Literary Theory published by Penguin* and Longman's *Advanced American Dictionary by Pearson/Longman* are among the source books. It is notable that the names of the source books are going to be addressed in their shortened forms throughout the thesis.

In this part, the researcher has only included those books and articles that play major roles in writing the thesis. There are some books or essays that their names have not been mentioned here as they have not been widely used for the sake of the thesis. It is befitting to be mentioned that articles and researches depend heavily on internet sources in the present time and this thesis is not an exception. The addresses of internet sources or the URLs will appear in the Bibliography section.

One of the requirements of writing a thesis is to introduce the dissertations that have been done with similar titles or related topics. The inquiries of the researcher indicate that no dissertations or theses are recorded or registered as the studies of the works of Zora Neale Hurston in the Iranian Research Institute for Information Science and Technology (IRANDOC) database until the time of accomplishing this section which was fall 2012. There was no record of a related dissertation in English Literature in Iran database in the time of the submission of the proposal which was winter 2010, either. However, searches are indicative of the existence of two articles fulfilled by Iranian researchers one of which is recorded in the Internal Journal of English and Literature, volume 3(4), April 2012, and appears on pages 84 to 90 with the title of "The Invisibility of I's in *Their Eyes Were Watching God*," accomplished by Mahmood Daram and Sepideh Hozhabrsadat in Shahid Chamran University of Ahvaz and accepted in the Academic Journals in 2012. The other article is presented by Fatemeh Azizmohammadi from the Islamic Azad University of Arak Branch and Nasser Mahmoudi from the Islamic Azad University of Shoushtar Branch in *2011 International Conference on Languages, Literature and Linguistics*, and published in *IPEDR volume 26* by *IACSIT Press* in 2011. Furthermore, there are many dissertations that explore works of Hurston and are recorded in foreign databases from the other countries especially the U.S.A. There is a master's diploma thesis that has also been a source of the present thesis, fulfilled by Jan Beneš in the department of English and American Studies of Masaryk University, Czech Republic, in 2012 with the title "Discourse on Sexuality in the Works of Zora Neale Hurston," found by means of Google search engine. Beneš debates how Hurston has created strong as well as complex characters within "Sweat," "Color Struck," *Their Eyes Were Watching God* and *Seraph on the Suwanee* by means of focusing on the Foucault's notion of sexuality.

"Janie's Journey: Language, body, and Desire in Zora Neale Hurston's *Their Eyes Were Watching God*" is the title of another master's degree thesis that has been accomplished by Yu-fen Lee from the National University of Sun Yat-Sen in June 2007. This thesis explores how women are marginalized within a male-dominated society by means of silencing their voices and repudiating their libidinal longings. Similar researches that are discovered in dissertations and theses section of ProQuest include: "Postcolonial African American female writers and their three-way battle against imperialism, canonization, and sexism: Developing a new multicultural feminism" by Damion Lewis in East Carolina University, 2010. It consists of 96 pages and was advised by Seodial F Deena. "A Feeling or Something More: "Love as a Liberating Force in *Their Eyes Were Watching God, Sula* and *The Women of Brewster Place*" is another related M.A research, written by Jennifer Matos Ayala in the University of Puerto Rico, Mayaguez (Puerto Rico), 2011. It consists of 101 pages and was advised by Jose M Irizarry Rodriguez. "Zora Neale Hurston and Alice Walker. Womanist and feminist theories meet in the garden: The perspective of difference" is the title of a Ph.D. dissertation by LaVie Totten Leasure from Indiana University of Pennsylvania. It was advised by Martha Bower, consists of 120 pages and was accomplished in 2005. Another Ph.D. dissertation which the researcher tracked as a similar thesis in ProQuest is "Why tell the truth when a lie will do? Re-creations and resistance in the self-authored life narratives of five American women fiction writers" by Piper G. Huguley from Georgia State University, submitted in 2006. It consists of 253 pages and was advised by Audrey Goodman. "Working it through: Women's working-class literature, the working-woman's body, and working-class pedagogy" is another related Ph.D. thesis by Cherie L. Rankin from Illinois State University, accomplished in 2007 with 273 pages and advised by Christopher D. Breu. "The black maternal: Heterogeneity and resistance in literary representations of black mothers in 20th century African American and Afro-Caribbean women's fiction" by Kinitra Dechaun Brooks from The University of North Carolina at Chapel Hill and fulfilled in 2008, "On speaking terms: Spirituality and sensuality in the tradition of modern black female intellectualism" by Shakira C. Holt from the University of Southern California in 2009 and "(Re)claiming self: Motive forces contributing to migration in African American literature by women" by Frances Dianne Henderson from Vanderbilt University accomplished in 2009 were among other related dissertations that the researcher could seek out in ProQuest database. The writer of this research could find the information of more related theses in WorldCat Database. *"Their eyes were watching God:* Janie Starks's search for identity and self-fulfillment", an M.A thesis by Emma Waters, "Heroes of marginality in Zora Neale Hurston's *Moses man of the mountain* and *Their eyes were watching God*" by Julie Ann Roemer, Women on women: the Black woman writer of the Harlem Renaissance By Deborah E McDowell, "Kissin'-friends : the women of Their eyes were watching God and Sula" by Patricia Williams Dougherty, "Circles of Sisterfriends : Women's Relationships in Three Black Women's Novels" by Hope White, "Writing the Body Across the Disciplines : Social Science and Literature, 1880-1940" by Christine Berni, "Claiming Ownership : Constructing Female Identity in *Their Eyes Were Watching God, Sula,* and *The Color Purple*" by Kimberly O Cox, ""She Pressed Her Teeth Together and Learned to Hush" : Janie's Silences in *Their Eyes Were Watching God*" by Meredith L Bailey "Jump at de Sun" : Rejecting Patriarchy and Conventionality in Zora Neale Hurston's *Their Eyes Were Watching God* and Alice Walker's *The Color Purple* by Tiffany M Harrington, "Defining Feminism : Defending Zora Neale Hurston's *Seraph on the Suwanee* as a Feminist Text" by Amani Hollins-Williams, "Talkin' in Rhymes : Language in Zora Neale Hurston's novels" by Joni Louise Johnson, "An Examination of the Emerging Feminist Voice in Zora Neale Hurston's *Their eyes Were Watching God* and Kate Chopin's *The Awakening*" by Fran Shultz, "Making the Invisible Visible: Women's Voice in Zora Neale Hurston's *Their eyes Where watching God* and "Sweat"" by Veanda L Hemphill and "Literacies of Resistance:

Script and Voice in Five Twentieth Century Women's Novels by Patricia Major Andres are among the most related results among 512 theses and dissertations that were recorded in WorldCat database.

1.4. Thesis Outline

In this section, a concise report about the following chapters is going to be given so that the readers can have an overview of what is going to happen and what they are going to be faced with while reading the thesis. This thesis consists of five chapters, the first of which is introduction. In this chapter, general information about the author of the selected novels, the goal of the research, major sources as well as a brief explanation of the next chapters, the approach and methodology and finally the definition of the technical jargons are revealed.

In chapter two, the thesis is going to put the selected approach under consideration. In this chapter, the researcher tries to introduce post-structuralist feminist literary theory and criticism. Starting with a brief and general introduction of feminism, the history of feminism and feminist literary criticism is put forward, as well. This chapter does not only focus on the main influential feminist figures, particularly Virginia Woolf and Simone de Beauvoir, but also provides a brief account of the post-structuralist and deconstructionist thinkers, specifically Derrida and Lacan. The researcher has decided to include these figures in order to demonstrate their impact on the current of post-structuralist feminist thought and their connection with Cixous.

After a brief introduction to feminism, its history and the influential thinkers, the thesis goes on to handle with the most reputable French post-structuralist feminist thinkers including Julia Kristeva, Luce Irigaray and Hélène Cixous. The rest of the chapter concentrates on the theories of Cixous, particularly her theory of écriture féminine. This thesis is concerned with the aspects, concepts and elements of feminine writing in order to study the selected texts.

Chapter three, with the heading of "Words Walking without Masters," analyzes two major aspects of feminine writing in Zora Neale Hurston's *Their Eyes Were Watching God* and *Seraph on the Suwanee*. The concepts that are being investigated in this chapter are concerned with plurality and openness. The researcher is going to inspect the evidences of these aspects within the texts. The elaborations are tried to be proven by means of excerpts from the novels. Occasionally, the researcher tries to prove her claims by means of direct quotations made by critics. As multiplicity or in other words; plurality is produced by different factors, the thesis attempts to introduce the factors that perform influential roles in producing plurality within the selected texts. These elements are mainly the literary figure; metaphor in the selected texts along with bisexuality and pun. The quality of openness which, to put it simply, means lack of repressive structure is going to be inspected in the texts, as well.

The heading of chapter four is: "I was born with all I ever needed to handle your case." This chapter investigates the concepts of body, voice and resisting patriarchy. Throughout this chapter, the notion of body is studied to find out how the heroines apply their bodies as weapons against the oppressive attitudes of patriarchal representatives. It also aims to review how voice helps the heroines of the selected novels to become emancipated from patriarchy and their inner repression. The existence of voice in the texts is going to be examined as well. This chapter is indeed going to study if different versions of patriarchy are resisted or dismantled within the novels.

Chapter five is the last chapter of the thesis. In this chapter the discussions in chapters three and four are being summed up. As a result, it is assumed whether Zora Neale Hurston's *Their Eyes Were Watching God* and *Seraph on the Suwanee* can be considered as models of écriture féminine. Furthermore, other problematic and questionable concepts within the selected texts, possible researches and approaches that could be performed on the works of Hurston are introduced there.

1.5. Approach and Methodology

The method that is applied by most of the researches in the field of literature is library-based. The current research has also benefited from library-based method in addition to the utilization of electronic sources. In order to accomplish the goals of this thesis, the researcher owes to books, different encyclopedias as well as various different essays and articles. The electronic sources range from different internet sites about the selected author or theoretician and the related theories to online archives, encyclopedias and indexes. Internet as a kind of electronic source has had a significant role in obtaining some articles, dissertations and books as well as information. This research is indebted to emails in order to gain information about selecting the approach and other similar matters. Major books and articles have been introduced briefly in literature review. The bibliography at the end of the thesis also contains the sources that this research is based on.

The approaches that the researcher has obtained to study Hurston's *Their Eyes Were Watching God* and *Seraph on the Suwanee* are post-structuralist and feminist approaches. Feminist studies is consisted of different trends and several approaches including: Marxist-feminist, Postmodern feminist, Post-colonialist feminist, psychoanalytic feminist, Post-structuralist feminist literary theory, etc. The approach that is chosen for this thesis is post-structuralist feminist theory and criticism. Some streaks of deconstruction are also mingled with it. This branch of feminism is highly dependent on post-structuralist thought because of its criticism of patriarchy and the means that it provides for literary analysis. This trend of thought has built its structures on Foucault's notions about knowledge, sexuality and reproductivity, and particularly Derridean theoretical issues about language as well as Lacanian psychoanalysis since they argued that in order to resist patriarchy it is "necessary not merely to think about new texts, but to think about them in radically new ways" (Richter 1432). Moreover they are concerned with the marginalized groups of people, especially women who are decentered under patriarchy as the patriarchal system of thought is structured upon hierarchies. The major post-structuralist feminists are Hélène Cixous, Monique Wittig, Luce Irigaray, Judith Butler and Julia Kristeva. Cixous, Kristeva, Irigaray and Wittig are known as French feminists as well. The focus of this research is to apply post-structuralist French feminist thought particularly Cixous's thoughts and theories on selected novels of Hurston.

Cixous is mostly concerned with writing as in the Western system of thought writing is the passive and thus negative side of the dual binary Speaking/Writing in the patriarchal binary oppositions series (Cixous, Clément 63). According to Richter "Cixous (following Derrida in *Of Grammatology*) sets up a series of binary oppositions (active/passive, sun/moon...father/mother, logos/pathos). Each pair can be analyzed as a hierarchy in which the former term represents the positive and masculine and the latter the negative and feminine principle" (1433-4). Cixous claims that all binary oppositions end in the binary couple Man/Woman in which Man is privileged over Woman and in this way dominates her. In her essay "Sorties", she writes that: "Either woman is passive or she does not exist" (Cixous, Clément 64). She demands dismantling of the binary oppositions. Cixous also appeals women to enter the site of writing and literary production that have been always reserved for men (*Signs* vol.1 876). In order to encourage women to write and break their silence, Cixous glorifies a feminine practice of writing which she calls "écriture féminine" or "writing the body" as well as writing in the "white ink."

Écriture féminine bears some distinctive features, the first of which is concentration on corporeality and physicality. The other trait of feminine writing is that it deals with the plural rather than singular. In other words, proliferation of meaning is momentous in écriture féminine. One of the clear characteristic of feminine writing is creativity. It also privileges openness and "otherness" (Eagleton, *Working* 182). Feminine modes of writing try to resist

27

patriarchy, break the silence and dismantle binary oppositions and imposed gender roles. This thesis concentrates on the notions of body, openness, multiplicity, resisting patriarchy and voice.

According to the adapted theoretical approach, a Reading Strategy is picked out by the researcher to study the literary texts. This Reading Strategy clarifies the steps that have been taken by the researcher. Before the application of the theories on the literary texts, some courses of reading of the novels are performed in advance. Some necessary researches about the author of the novels; Zora Neale Hurston as well as her attitudes and methods that have to be conducted have been done in advance. After studying about the theory the processes of analyzing the texts can be categorized.

The first step that the researcher has taken is to examine the multiplicity in the texts. As one of the tools of the production of plural meanings is the use of literary figures such as metaphor and pun, a close reading has to be performed in order to find examples that are metaphoric and to mention them in the report. Another influential factor to be taken into consideration is the issue of bisexuality of either the author or the heroines. Although bisexuality seems to bear connection with resistance toward the patriarchal gender roles, it impacts plurality as it multiplies the representations of gender within the texts which inevitably ends in the possibility of multiple representations. In this way, the researcher tries to prove the deferral of meaning.

The second step in order to accomplish the goals of this chapter is to examine whether there is an emphasis on openness within the texts or not. An open text does not rely on grammatical structures in a serious effective manner. It has a kind of circular form in which there are numerous repetitions while there seems to be no beginning or end. There is also the possibility of the existence and the coinage of inventory words and phrases. Thus, this mode of writing does not imitate or mimic masculine and male-dominated texts that attempt to be logical and imitate the accepted rules of writing as much as possible. A feminine text riots against the standard system of writing that is imposed on writers and obliges them to obey its rules, norms and standard values. The researcher should be careful to inspect and find these points within the selected texts.

The concepts of body, gaining voice and resisting patriarchy are dealt with throughout chapter four of the current thesis. First of all, there is an examination of the notion of the body within the novel by means of concentrating on the demonstration of longings and the author's attitude toward revealing it in the flow of her writing. The excerpts from the novels help to illustrate *jouissance* and women's erotic dreams. The scrutiny of the role of body as a device to attack patriarchy and capitalism is another notable aim of this chapter. The reader's being careful about the longings that have been repressed or hidden in the texts is obligatory as well.

In order to prove the deconstruction of patriarchy, the researcher has to recognize if any binary oppositions, that reinforce oppressions or gender constructions are resisted. One means of resistance is breaking the silence and starting to speak. The marginal character's attitude toward gaining voice and speech will be studied in the discussion about voice. The thesis tries to attain if the major characters in the narrative gain voice. In addition the researcher has to concentrate on the dialogues and see whether the text consists of as much dialogues as narration. Furthermore, the courage of the heroines and other female characters to speak in front of men and other domineering characters has to be explored.

The last step of studying the selected texts under the light of Cixous's post-structuralist feminism is to collect the resultant findings of the investigations and the examinations performed in chapters two, three and four. The outcome will clarify whether the texts of *Their Eyes Were Watching God* and *Seraph on the Suwanee* are considered as écriture feminine or not.

1.6. Definition of Terms

Androgyny: According to Sarah Gamble's *The Routledge Companion to Feminism and Postfeminism*, androgyny is a Greek word produced from the combination of '"andro'" which means male and '"gyn'" which means female (150-1). Androgyny is the fluid distribution of characteristics of both genders in an individual. It has been a seminal concept for feminists because it has a liberating potential. Virginia Woolf announces androgyny as a necessary element of artistic expression (Gamble 151). Woolf believes that an artist should be "womanly-manly" or "manly-womanly" (Cited in Gamble 151). Another signal side of Woolf's androgyny, according to Gamble, is its attempts to deconstruct the duality of gender classification (151).

Binary Oppositions: Appeared as "Binary operations" in Bressler's *Literary Criticism* (334), the term binary simply means '"composed of two'" and '"twofold'" (Cuddon 82). Language is made of numerous and countless binary oppositions, for example: "up/down; slow/fast; sense/nonsense; truth/falsehood; black/white; man/woman – and so on" (82). This concept has a central role in structuralist studies. It gives hierarchy, order and centering to the context. In contrast to structuralism, post-structuralism tries to dismantle binary oppositions and resist hierarchies as they "oversimplify meaning" (Cuddon 83). This term entered the field of literary theory and criticism by Derrida. He expresses his disapproval of "conceptual oppositions" and the Western metaphysics that is based upon them since Plato's time (Bressler 122).

Bisexuality: Being a primary element in French Feminist thought, particularly in Cixous's theories, it can also refer to a situation in which an individual enjoys both heterosexual and homosexual sources of pleasure (Gamble 159). In *The Newly Born Woman*, however, Cixous talks of bisexuality as "a fantasy of a complete being, which replaces the fear of castration" or "the location within oneself of the presence of both sexes" (Cixous, Clément 84-5). This idea of bisexuality refutes the phallocentric view of woman as 'Other' and the binary oppositions that are based on Man/Woman dualism. According to Gamble, bisexuality does not mean that genders are simply blended into each other, so the term or the concept does not refute the difference between them and is plural and playful, as a consequence (159). Cixous adds more to her theory of bisexuality by claiming woman as bisexual as she has not been trained like a man for "glorious phallic monosexuality" (Cixous, Clément 85).

Deconstruction: According to Cuddon, it is "a method of criticism" and a way of reading the texts (209). It is also the most significant concept of post-structuralism. According to Barbara Johnson, deconstruction is not related to "'destruction'" (Cuddon, 209). It means "'to undo'" and "'analysis'" as well, according to her. This method of reading and analysis argues that a text contains of numerous and different meanings and is not limited to one. Thus, there is no fixed central meaning as "texts deconstruct themselves" (Cuddon 210).

Différance: This term contains the capacity to be translated as both 'difference' and 'deferral'. Jacques Derrida, the proposer of this term believed that the structures of thought are built upon the binary oppositions in which one pole of the binary opposition is privileged over the other and defines it. Différance has been presented to refute the existing dual system of thought by resisting closure within the text as well as the existence of an ultimate meaning. Hélène Cixous has adapted this notion to apply it on her own notion of écriture féminine. Feminine writing bears the quality of excess and tries to dismantle binary oppositions upon which the symbolic order is structured.

Desire: According to Sarah Gamble, this concept is originated from Freud's theories of "'penis envy'" and "'castration complex'" (183). In his theories, Freud has represented women as "incomplete men" (Gamble, 183). This representation is based on the notion of 'lack' that women experience upon entering into the symbolic order and are obliged to identify with absent phallus instead of their present libidinal organ (Gamble, 183). As it is written in Sarah

31

Gamble's *Feminism and Postfeminism*, in the Symbolic Order males are the delegates of "the Name of the Father" while females are left dreaming up with the deprived phallus. In this respect, woman becomes the male's other who experiences lack and a female kind of desire. To compensate the lack, she is made to become the male's 'object of desire' which results in her estrangement from self. French feminists have not neglected to apply and rework the concept of female desire in their theories.

Écriture Féminine: This concept has been proposed by the French feminist Hélène Cixous. It is also called 'feminine writing' or 'writing the body'. Feminine writing has got characteristics which femininity of language, style of writing, tone and feeling are among them. Its language is completely different from male language (Cuddon 248). However, it has nothing to do with biological gender. As it is written in Cixous's *The Laugh of the Medusa*, men are capable of practicing feminine writing, as well. Cixous recognizes 'mother' as the source of feminine writing and thinks that a person who practices it writes in the "white ink" (*Signs* vol.1 No.4 881). In such a kind of writing, logic is subverted and there is a free play of meaning.

On the other hand, Irigaray proposes "woman's language" that is characterized by multiplicity, fluidity and diversity (Gamble 190). It is heterogeneous in addition to being resistant to phallocentrism. According to Sarah Gamble's *Feminism and Postfeminism*, Irigaray's theory of "woman's language" is relied on "the shape and structure of the genital organs"(190).

Essentialism: This term is related to the concept of gender. It denotes "natural or innate differences between men and women" and insists on its state of natural and fixed beings in contrast to some feminist and gender studies thinkers who think that gender is a social and cultural construct (Gamble 192).

Gender: It is considered as a social construction. Psychoanalytic feminists in contrast to some thinkers such as Judith Butler put no difference between sex and gender and believe that they are intertwined (Gamble 209).

Female: Literally, it points to an individual who has got certain biological features, one of which is the ability to give birth. In this respect, it is different from 'femininity' which is a social construct. However, feminists try to posit a definition of female that surpasses her productive system. Unfortunately, in the Western system of thought, 'female' has got a negative meaning because of being the inferior to 'male' in the binary opposition Male/Female and thus it is regarded as passive (Gamble 198). Post-structuralism has tried to resist the binary oppositions including the binary opposition Male/Female. Post-structuralist feminists try to refute the conventional definitions of femaleness and connect it with artistic creation and writing practice. Gamble writes that for both Cixous and Irigaray: "the biological female body functions as a highly stylized metaphor which represents the point from which female knowledge can be produced" (198).

Femininity: While femaleness is the result of biological matters, femininity is the product of cultural structures. According to Gamble, femininity could be regarded as a series of rules that control one's female structure and it aims at women's submission to be the male's 'object of desire'. However, these definitions do not apply in French. In French, the word 'féminine' has got both of the mentioned meanings within itself. In the field of Cixousian and Kristevan theories, femininity has got a vaster meaning. It represents "all that is marginalized within the patriarchal order, and is thus a term which describes a position that can be occupied by any peripheral subject, be they male or female" (Gamble 1990).

Imaginary: It is derived from Lacan's reworking of Freud's theories. It starts with a phase in which the child recognizes no difference between his/her body and the mother's body. It also consists of a narcissistic stage in which the child identifies with its own image. This phase is

33

called "mirror stage" and is characterized with narcissism (Cixous, Clément 165). When the identity is involved in the process of evolution, the child becomes separated from her mother's body and starts to feel being an individual (Gamble 225). French women writers such as Cixous assert on the relationship with the mother's body in the pre-Oedipal stage or in other words the Imaginary. Cixous searches for "a feminine imaginary" which employs the unity with the maternal body (Gamble 255).

Logocentrism: According to Cuddon, it is a term coined by Jacques Derrida. Although it literally means "'centred on the word,'" Derrida believes that it involves the whole system of thought which relies on the "desire for truth"(477). In Derrida's point of view, philosophy revolves around the element of logocentrism since Plato (Cuddon 477).

Metaphor: It is the basic figure in poetry. By means of metaphor, an implicit comparison could be made, whereas the comparison resulted from simile is explicit (Cuddon 507). Metaphor, as Jalal Sokhanvar states, "is a figure of language which omits the comparative term (like, as, than) and says or implies, that one thing is another that cannot be" (55).

Other/other: According to Lacanian theories, by making the other as one's own influential part, the ego will be produced. In another respect, all cultures recognize themselves in comparison and relation to those cultures that they are not. Those cultures are considered as their Other. Betsy Wing, the translator of *The Newly Born Woman* writes that when 'other' is spelled with small "o", it refers generally to an experiential matter, while with a capital "O"; it has mostly a theoretical connotation. In some contexts, the 'Other' can refer to what is repressed or the Law that represses it (Cixous, Clément 167).

Phallocentrism: It basically conveys a system which is centered on the symbolic phallus and points to a culture in which phallus is the privileged element, thus it turns to be a "transcendental signified" and the highest symbol of power. This term has a large application in feminist studies and is applied by critics such as Cixous and Kristeva in their attempts to deconstruct patriarchal constructions such as the binary oppositions (Cuddon 662).

Phallogocentric: This term has been also invented by Derrida and is a combination of 'phallocentric' and 'logocentric'. It is exploited to point to a system or society which imposes power by means of sexual form of social influence. According to Cuddon, post-structuralists present "modern Western societies as phallogocentric novels in which male characters have the upper hand and female characters are sex objects"(662).

Propre: It is translated as "Selfsame" in *The Newly Born Woman* (Cixous, Clément 78,167). Selfsame can be the synonym of "ownself" and it has connotations of appropriation, possession and property (167). According to Betsy Wing, the translator of *The Newly Born Woman* it also means "proper" and "clean" (167).

Pun: According to Cuddon, it is a figure of speech which implies "a play upon words" (711). It is considered as one of the earliest sorts of wordplay. It has a wide usage and produces humor (Cuddon 711).

Symbolic: It is the order of language and one enters it when he/she is introduced to language. Lacan prefers it to other phases because it represents both the Imaginary and the Real phases. When one enters the Symbolic order by means of learning the language and the abstractions, he/she gets free from the Imaginary. These abstractions are: "The name (*nom*) and the prohibition (*non*) of the father" and they lead the child to find his/her position in the cultural structure. According to Betsy Wing, the power of the abstractions is originated from "the threat of castration as signified by the phallus." Although it is controlled by patriarchy, Cixous sees women's lively entry into language as the only way to free them from being objects and help them to become subjects (Cixous, Clément 168).

Subjectivity: Traditionally, 'ego' and 'self' can be considered as the synonyms of subject. In liberal humanism subject is one who has been granted with the power of reason and thus has a unique identity. Postmodern thought has in fact tried to undermine the traditional and liberalist visions of subjectivity. Therefore, subject is not the conscious individual who produces language but is regarded as the receiver of it. Postmodernism and Kristevan post-structuralism has offered the notion of "subject in process" (Gamble 307). Feminists, however, claim that female subjectivity is defined by patriarchy in all its linguistic, social and biological respects as the result of the female subject's entry into the Symbolic order and the privilege of phallus in this phase. Therefore, female subject is recognized by her lack of penis and identified by means of her difference.

CHAPTER TWO

Post – structuralist Feminist Criticism and Hélène Cixous

2.1. Introduction

What is feminine? And what is écriture féminine? How is it different from a feminist text? What are the seminal signs and factors of écriture féminine? Who is the founder of this form of writing? Is it influenced by other thinkers? Why feminine writing and its founders are categorized under feminist literary criticism? What is a feminine reading? How should a text be read femininely? What are the techniques to read a text in the light of this form of criticism? In other words, when the notion of feminine writing is being spoken about, what are the issues, elements and factors that should be considered? On whom theories are the discussions in this chapter based? These are the basic, fundamental and necessary questions that are going to be dealt and worked with throughout this chapter. Throughout the next two chapters the texts of *Their Eyes Were Watching God* and *Seraph on the Suwanee* are going to be worked out, based on the notions discussed throughout this chapter. Before going through the notions under discussion, a brief and general introduction to feminist literary criticism is going to be presented.

2.2. Feminism

According to Merriam-Webster online dictionary, feminism is a general term to define a political, cultural or economic movement with the aim of maintaining women's rights in all aspects of life and providing their legal and social protection. It also includes issues of gender difference, women's rights and interests that led to the establishment of movements and campaigns to gain them. Although almost everybody thinks that feminism is just a revolutionary activity to gain equal power and rights or liberation for women to the utmost, it

37

is not limited to these points. According to Bressler, some feminist intellectuals such as Toril Moi think that feminist criticism is a theoretical, political, and critical approach to dismantle patriarchy within all cultural areas (Cited in Bressler, 168). However, the recent feminist criticism have found their theoretical basis in the Lacanian and Derridean trends of poststructuralist thinking in order to escape the fixed theories and intellectual frames. In addition, they are aiming at developing a female discourse that does not belong to the male-dominated system of language production. In this way, they have not only refused "the masculine notion of authority or truth," but they can articulate the subversive and "formless resistance" of female intellectuals to male literary discourse (Selden, Widdowson 204). Furthermore, the definition of feminism in its details and different related studies is far vaster and much more complicated. It is divided into three major historical phases and about thirteen "'petits recits'" that are grounded in special cultural-political arenas: "Marxist-feminist, black and African, Asian, women-of-color, American, French, Irish, black-British, gynocritics, gynesis, psychoanalytic, myth, 'Third-World'/Third-Wave, deconstructive and lesbian-feminist" (Selden, Widdowson 205- 6). French feminism could be added to these categories, as well. As could be recognized, the field of feminist critical theories is contained of particular dynamically "'open'" and problematizing discourses and discussions (Selden, Widdowson 206). The historical phases of feminist literary criticism are divided into three waves officially: First Wave, Second Wave and Third Wave.

2.2.1. Historical Background

Women's exploitation and discrimination has a long history which reaches ancient Greek in Western culture. They thought that women do not let men search for truth by means of enticing them (Bressler 171). Some like Aquinas went further to address them as "'imperfect man'" as cited in *A Reader's Guide to Contemporary Literary Theory* (Selden, Widdowson

203). Even in the later Europe there were thinkers like Darwin who regarded women as their inferior not just physically but also intellectually (Bressler 171).

Through time women have started to raise their voices in order to shiver the roots of patriarchy. The first challenging feminist work that has been written in the late fourteenth century is Christine de Pisan's *Epistre au Dieu D'amours* (Bressler 171). In her *La Cite Des Dames,* Pisan declares men and women as equal creatures of God (Bressler 171). Another influential feminist voice to blur patriarchy was echoed in the late eighteenth century by Mary Wollstonecraft who has written *A Vindication of the Rights of Women.* However, the major impressing feminist voices have not been introduced to the world until the twentieth century.

The modern feminism is divided into two major waves or phases, followed by a third one, which is almost postmodernist in its tendencies and trends. The crucial factors that developed the First Wave Feminism are Women's Rights and Women's Suffrage movements because they have emphasized political, economic and social improvements for women. The significant figures of this era are Virginia Woolf and Simone de Beauvoir.

2.2.2. Virginia Woolf

Mary Eagleton regards Virginia Woolf as "the founding *mother* of the contemporary debate" since she has presented many issues that later feminists are concerned with (Cited in Selden, Widdowson 207). Her most critical and influential texts in their feminist concern are *A Room of One's Own* (1929) and *Three Guineas* (1938). Woolf's main involvement, like other first wave feminists, is with women's material limitations compared to men. While *A Room of One's Own* focuses on the historical and social atmosphere of women's literary production, the second mentioned book focuses on the relations between male power and professions such as law, medicine and education (Selden, Widdowson 207). Although Woolf believed that women have always encountered with social and economic obstacles in the course of their literary productions, she asked for a neutral femininity, which is not concerned with the notion of femaleness or maleness. Woolf believed in androgyny and a withdrawal from the conflict of maleness and femaleness (Selden, Widdowson 207).

Furthermore, according to Toril Moi's *Sexual/Textual Politics*, Woolf has a "deconstructive" and therefore Derridean practice of writing. Woolf's texts demonstrate the dishonest and deceitful nature of discourse in Moi's opinion by means of uncovering the way through which language repudiates the presentation of clear and definite meaning. Moreover, she exposes the way in which language is not reduced to a certain unified meaning. She considers the search for a fixed essential meaning as a "metaphysical" attempt (Moi 9). From Derridean perspective, there is an endless "freeplay of signifiers" that "'will never yield a final, unified meaning'" (Moi 9). Woolf's purpose of grasping such a playful and sensual language is perhaps an attempt to undermine the phallogocentric ideology that tries to rule by means of its logocentric and teleological equipment.

Hélène Cixous, the French post-structuralist feminist, on whose ideas and theories this thesis is chiefly founded upon, has some affinities with Virginia Woolf. Similar to Woolf who is concerned with the notion of androgyny and is against maleness or femaleness, Cixous favors the bisexuality within both the writer and reader as "the location within oneself of the presence of both sexes" (Cixous, Clément *The Newly* 85). Moreover, both Cixous and Woolf prefer and practice texts, which produce proliferated meaning by means of metaphors, puns and parodies, deconstruction and deferral of meaning.

2.2.3. Simone de Beauvoir

Simone de Beauvoir is in reality on the margin of the first wave and the second wave feminism. One of the most unique feminists of all time, Beauvoir was the forever partner of Jean Paul Sartre and the founder of the newspaper *Nouvelle féministes* and the feminist theory journal *Questions feminists* (Selden, Widdowson 209). She has also been a women's rights activist. Her major book *The Second Sex* that has been published in 1949 is involved with the fundamental questions on modern feminism. It is not based on the traditional Marxist theory but on existentialist philosophy of Jean Paul Sartre (Moi, 90). Beauvoir also founded the journal *Questions féministes* in 1977 with the cooperation of some other women such as Christine Delphy (Selden, Widdowson 209). It was established in order to make a forum especially for different socialist and anti-essentialist forms of feminism.

In her work *The Second Sex*, De Beauvoir distinguishes between sex and gender and declares that: "One is not born, but rather becomes a woman" and "it is civilization as a whole that produces this creature" or "Only the intervention of someone else can establish an individual as an *other*" (Cited in Moi, 90). Thus, she makes highly serious distinctions between "'being female'" and being produced as "'a woman'" (Selden, Widdowson 210). She regards woman as a social construct. Like other first-wave feminists, she seeks freedom from biological difference and recognition of women's rational abilities in society.

2.2.4. Second Wave Feminism

In the field of feminist literary theory, second-wave feminism is divided by some scholars into two major branches of Anglo-American feminist criticism and French feminist theory though this national division of feminist theory seems not appealing to some other scholars. Anglo-American feminism is mostly supported by Elaine Showalter's gynocriticism, which aims at recovering the tradition of women authors and examining women's own culture. The opposite of this trend is the so-called French feminism that does not concentrate on the gender of the author but on the effect of writing. However, the names of these critical movements are troublesome because there might be many American and English critical thinkers who might be entitled French because of the critical field that they belong to. Therefore, the investigation of intellectual tradition of the feminist thinkers is noteworthy not their nationality. The other flaw of such a categorization is that it is believed to be inadequate in exploring the Black or

41

Women-of-color and Queer literary theories. It also seems to exclude the feminist literary theory of the other areas such as the Third-World (Selden, Widdowson 211-13).

The major Anglo-American literary theory figures are: Kate Millet, Eva Figes, Shulamith Firestone, Germaine Greer, Mary Ellman, Michèle Barrett, Cora Kaplan, Elaine Showalter, Sandra Gilbert and Susan Gubar. On the other hand, the so-called French feminist criticism or more appropriate to call it post-structuralist feminist criticism is almost influenced by the works of Julia Kristeva, Hélène Cixous and Luce Irigaray. This key strand of the second wave feminism is just originated from France and has no national boundary.

While deriving from de Beauvoir's concept of "Other" which perceives woman as the "Other" to man, post-structuralist French feminism has roots and backgrounds in the theories of Lacan and Derrida. Gender, class and race are identified as binary oppositions, for example: man/woman, Black/White and middle class/working class. As the result of these binary oppositions, differences are brought up among groups of people, which cause one group to oppress or dominate the other (Selden, Widdowson 222). French feminists' aim is to find a way to break down these male-dominated and conventional stereotypes of sexual difference by means of focusing on language, the result of which is the production of "women's language" (Selden, Widdowson 222). Since, post-Structuralist feminism is deeply rooted in the psychoanalysis of Lacan, it would be more suitable to review it briefly. Moreover, as Lacan, Derrida and others are influential post-structuralist thinkers and critics, this review will be commenced by an introduction from post-structuralism.

2.3. Post-structuralism

Post-structuralism is indeed a byproduct of structuralism that appeared in the late 1960s. It tries to refute structuralism's attempt to see the intellectual world in the form of an organized system of "artificial signs" (Selden, Widdowson 125). Selden and Widdowson approve the relation between post-structuralists and structuralists by stating: "Poststructuralists are structuralists who suddenly see the error of their ways" (125).

While humanists believe that they can understand the outside world by means of their rational minds, structuralists view language as the producer of reality through which one may think. In the humanist mode of thinking the "self" is the center of meaning whereas in the structuralist model the source of meaning is language. Post-structuralists, on the other hand, question the humanist model of human "subject" or "self". The post-structuralist human subject is fragmented and therefore not unified. There is no center in a post-structuralist system including a human subject. Thus, human subject is regarded as a location of different cultural constructs. Furthermore, post-structuralism introduces the concept of "subject in process" or the "speaking subject" instead of structuralism's "subjects" that are produced by linguistic systems (Selden, Widdowson 127).

In post-structuralism as well as structuralism, everything starts from Saussure's linguistic theory. In his theory, "langue" is the system, structure and organization of language, whereas "parole" is its superstructure consisted of one's speech and writing. Signifier and signified are two sides of a coin without any necessary connection (Selden, Widdowson 125). There can be a signifier for two signifieds or one signifier for one signified. The meaning is produced by differences of sounds combined with differences of ideas, according to Saussure. He also adds that one signified is able to seek its own signifier by means of a natural tendency (Cited in Selden, Widdowson, 126). However, post-structuralists assert "the *unstable* nature of signification" (Selden, Widdowson, 126). Therefore, there is no linguistic coherence in the post-structuralist model.

Jacques Derrida and Jacques Lacan are two significant post-structuralist figures that have had an extraordinary impact on post-structuralist French feminist thinkers and critics. Derrida thinks that the Western metaphysics is defined in terms of dualistic oppositions within which

43

one term takes the dominant position over the other. The dominant terms are always positive while the subordinated ones are negative. The inferior term is defined by means of the dominant term. The system which is consisted of these binary oppositions is hierarchical. There is one ultimate truth in a hierarchical system and as strucuralists offer, one center. Thus, Derrida has coined the term "Logocentrism" to point to such structures of thought and culture. Derrida's goal is to deconstruct this "logocentric" structure of binary oppositions in which limited fixed meanings are produced by means of the difference between the binaries. Moi writes: "For Derrida, meaning (signification) is not produced in the static closure of binary opposition. Rather it is achieved through the "free play of the signifier"" (104). The "open-ended play between the presence of one signifier and the absence of others" is the fundamental origin of Derrida's "différance" (Moi 104). This term is translated as "difference" in addition to "deferral" in English, which suggests that there is no one ultimate meaning because of "the interplay between presence and absence" (Moi, 104). Cixous is similar to Derrida, in her concern for an open text in which there is a "free play of the signifier" in addition to her insistence on the refutation of binary oppositions (Moi 106).

Lacan has reworked the theories of Freud but has tried to create a new system of thought (Sarup 7). He has had a significant influence on French poststructuralist feminism. He perceives the infant's entry into the culture by means of its identification with its own mirror image. In this phase, the child perceives itself as a separate being (Gamble 25). The child's entry into the Symbolic Order is by means of the acquisition of language. According to Lacan, the Symbolic order is patriarchal because of its construction of meaning via binary oppositions, in which the "male" is always privileged over the "female" (Gamble 25). The Law of the Father with phallus as its favored signifier is opposed to the realm of the mother or the Imaginary in which every desire is satisfied and the child perceives itself as a separate being. Lacan views the position of "woman" in the Symbolic as founded on "Lack" or

44

"Absence," so that "woman" cannot identify with the Phallus (Gamble 25). As a consequence she is on the edge of the Symbolic because she is not completely supported by the system of language and becomes marginal.

Whereas Saussure implies that human beings are outside language, Lacan insists that human subjects are caught in everyday language and cannot escape from it (Sarup10). As a result, the only access to others is through language and a person who does not know what language is, is regarded as a "psychotic" (Sarup 10). Moreover, both Lacan and Cixous believe that words can convey plural meanings and they are used to signify something different from their substantial meanings. Lacan thinks that this is due to human being's "metaphoric ability," hence he insists on the autonomous system of signifiers (Sarup 9).

2.3.1. Post-structuralist Feminism

During the post-structuralist and postmodernist era, as a result of feminism's understanding of the notions of sensuality, gender, race and class, the theorization of subjectivity have been extended. This caused feminism to approve post-structuralist approaches such as deconstruction. Post-structuralist feminists try to challenge phallocentrism and seek to improve new feminine and masculine perspectives together.

For feminist critical theory with a post-structuralist outlook, "the site of cultural production of identity" is language. Therefore, instead of stable gender identities, there are changeable identities due to the discourse and there are speaking "gendered subjects" instead of individuals (Gamble 115). Post-structuralist feminist theoreticians seek to find out how gender is created within the structure of language. They examine how subjects are gendered as "man" or "woman," or masculine and feminine through following Lacan.

Although post-structuralist French feminists bear numerous differences from each other, they have one common feature. This characteristic is that all of them including Kristeva, Irigaray and Cixous have been influenced by Lacanian Psychoanalysis. Another common

45

characteristic is their interesting notions and statements "about subjectivity, sexuality, language and desire" (Sarup 109). Lacan's view of a linguistic construction of biological difference has influenced these deconstructionist French feminist theorists. Irigaray, Kristeva and Cixous strive for a new female identity, writing and language to subvert "the Phallocentricity of the Symbolic Order" (Gamble 34). As a result of this, they have established new methods to study "the relationship between desire and language" (Gamble 34).

The main facets of Hélène Cixous's work are her hostility toward what is called "patriarchal binary oppositions". She opposes to hierarchical and dualistic thoughts. In addition, she declares for a feminine practice of writing, which is closely connected to the body. Cixous views feminine sensuality as multiple and resourceful. She thinks that feminine libido and writing are connected to each other. Therefore, feminine writing could be considered as a means to subvert patriarchy.

Irigaray believes that women suffer from repression via language because they live in a world that is governed by patriarchal language. Women perform the role of reflecting the masculinity of western male philosophers. Although she is dedicated to Freud, she thinks that Freud "was projecting the masculine fear of castration onto women when he hypothesized that women suffer from penis envy, that they have been castrated" (Tyson 101). She also perceives patriarchal order in what is called "male gaze." It conveys that men have to look and women have to be looked at (Tyson 102). Thereupon, man is in the position of control because he sees and woman is reduced to be an object. Like Cixous, Irigaray views the means of woman's emancipation from patriarchy in language. She is in favor of women only group and the notion of women's language which she calls "womanspeak" (Tyson 102). Similar to Cixous, who locates the source of feminine writing in the feminine body, Irigaray considers the source of "womanspeak" in the female body (Tyson 102). Thereupon, "womanspeak" is as proliferating and as diversified as écriture féminine.

In contrast, Kristeva does not believe in any particular woman's language such as "écriture féminine" or "womanspeak." She believes that "feminine" is a term that is not definable because there is as much feminine as there are women (Tyson 103). Furthermore, she sees the differences between men and women as sets of social differences rather than biological differences. She also affirms that both men and women can pass the patriarchal language by means of what she calls "semiotic" which is quite in contrast with the symbolic (Tyson 103). Semiotic, as cited in Tyson's *Critical Theory Today*, consists of intonation, rhythm and body language, hence it can be conveyed as the way one speaks (103). Although Kristeva agrees with Irigaray and Cixous on the exclusion of femaleness from the site of subject, she approaches the question of subjectivity from a different perspective that leads her to analyze the oppression of women successfully. Furthermore, she has presented a possible path of emancipation by means of replacing dynamism instead of essence. Kristeva exploits substantial Lacanian and Derridean concepts. She refuses to accept Freud's model of the ego as a universal subject that existed before. She is quite the opposite of Lacan that considers subject, gender and sensuality as linguistic constructs and not biological ones (Moi, 96). Unlike Cixous who has romanticized "female's body as the site of woman's writing," Kristeva's major involvement is to hypothesize a revolution which relies on gender, class and "construction of femininity" (Moi 96). In fact, Kristeva has got common ideas with Beauvoir. Like Kristeva, Irigaray is very similar to Beauvoir in her attitude toward criticizing woman's repression in phallogocentric discourse. To some extent, Irigaray does "a post-structuralist rewriting of Beauvoir's analysis of woman as man's Other" (Moi 96).

Although the aforementioned post-structuralist French feminists are not regarded as feminist critics by their counterparts, they have had an exceptional influence on the discussion of women's repression and their resistance toward patriarchy. It is notable that even some of these post-structuralist thinkers such as Cixous and Kristeva do not regard themselves as feminists. Their complicated intellectualism led them to be disregarded by the Anglo-American feminists (Moi 86). Post-structuralist French feminism is highly indebted to and mingled with the continental philosophy. Furthermore, their attitude to work on the different linguistic, textual, psychoanalytic and semiotic issues adds to the abstract quality of their theories. However, the researcher believes that they can be categorized as feminist critics due to their urgent attempts to dismantle the patriarchal order and introduction of the recoverable new gender modes and concepts. Moi convincigly adds that: "French theory has contributed powerfully to the feminist debate about the nature of women's oppression, the construction of sexual difference and the specificity of women's relation's to language and writing" (94).

As the main focus of this research is the application of Hélène Cixous's theories, the rest of this chapter is going to be allocated to her writings and arguments as well as their applicability. Through the next two chapters, the Cixousian approach will be adapted to study the selected texts in order to reach the research's objectives. Cixous's intellectual and political background is introduced throughout the next discussion. The introduction of her background will be followed by an investigation of her theories.

2.3.2. Cixous's Intellectual and Political Background

Hélène Cixous is the author of novels, plays, short stories and essays. In addition to being a radical feminist, in spite of her own rejection of this term, she is a philosopher, professor, poet, a literary scholar and a rhetorician. She is the professor of English Literature at the University of Paris VIII-Vincennes and has established the first center for women's studies in Europe in that university. She is a co-founder of the journal "Poetique," as well. Thinkers that have had impact on Cixous are Jacques Derrida, Sigmund Freud, Jacques Lacan and Martin Heidegger. She has debated the works of Heinrich Von Kleist, Franz Kafka, Arthur Rimbaud,

Clarice Lispector, Maria Rilke, Paul Celan, Jean Genet, Osip Mandelstam, Marina Tsvetva, James Joyce, Anna Akhmatova, E.T.A Hoffman, Friedrich Hölderlin and William Shakespeare within her different articles and considers their selected works as suitable instances of feminine writing (Sellers xxx). As mentioned previously, like other post-structuralist French feminists, she is influenced by Lacan, Derrida and definitely Freud.

Cixous's most influential and recognized essays are: *La Jeune Née* or *The Newly Born Woman,* written in 1975 in collaboration with Catherine Clément, "Le Rire de la Méduse" (1975), the translation of which appeared in 1976 as "The laugh of Medusa," "le Sexe Ou La tête?" (1976), translated as "Castration or Decapitation?"(1981). *La Venue à l'écriture* (1977) is her other work which is translated as "Coming to Writing" and is printed with some other essays.

Like Irigaray and Kristeva, Cixous's work is based on Jacques Lacan's theories. Cixous seems to be optimistic about the possibilities of the Pre-Oedipal phase where she locates écriture féminine which is for her a method to challenge the Law of the Father. She rejects the binary oppositions of the Symbolic mode that silence women. In contrary to Freud who considers women as having lack, Cixous proclaims women's possession of excess. Cixous uses the case of Dora and her hysteria in one of her plays as a speaking body that threatens patriarchy, since Dora's words seem to rebel against the main author of her story. In general, the strategies of theorists like Cixous are at odds with the biological readings of Freud. They all reflect the notion of femininity. Feminine writing is based on culturally achieved conventions not on an available essence of male and female characteristics. One of the sought notions could be the "openness" in the feminine texts as a lack of repressive patterning. Some questions that have been always raised by these cultural revolutionists are: How is power deployed by writing? How to read a feminine text? And what the feminine is? Her essays "The Laugh of the Medusa" and "Castration or Decapitation?" are among Cixous's demonstrations against some psychoanalytical myth in reading the feminine. She describes how the structure of writing is formed from a gender-specific position that favors men and how it works to gain profit for the male by reducing writing to the Law of the Father and the Symbolic order.

Cixous's autobiographical writings stress on her own sense of not belonging to the numerous cultures and led her to focus on the notion of "Otherness." So, écriture féminine is considered as an escape from the religious, biological, linguistic and cultural oppressions (Eagleton, *Working* 154). Cixous is fighting the limitations surrounding and fighting her as "Other." The title of her essay "Sorties/Out and Out/Attacks/Ways Out/Forays" proves the previously mentioned fact very well. In "Sorties" the notions of women's desires and language are under inspection.

In "The Laugh of the Medusa" Greek myth is combined with its psychoanalytic mythology in order to challenge the current patriarchal beliefs. Her writing is not completely theoretical. Cixous challenges the boundaries between theory and fiction. She aims to liberate women's bodies from the existing regulations and representations by means of erotic images, syntax, puns and fluidity in writing. Cixous recognizes patriarchy as a historical and cultural context built out of power relations. They exist in reality and are not separate from the aesthetics and poetics ("Hélène Cixous and the Rhetoric of Feminine Desire").

Writing is a practice with unique opportunities for feminist politics. Along with flourishing from the body, it is culturally and ideologically determined. Cixous's introduction of the notion of "écriture feminine" and its possibilities has some shortcomings. It does not point to the material issues that prevent women from writing. According to Moi, it mentions "nothing of the actual inequities, deprivations and violations that women, as social beings rather than as mythological archetypes, must constantly suffer" (Moi 123).

After 1968, there have been feminist critics who wished to make a connection between politics and psychoanalysis. The *Psyche et Po* was an active foundation that rejected feminism. The interrelation between theory and practice resulted in recognition of women's own internal phallocentrism to make a distinctive powerful trend of feminism as their enemy. Hélène Cixous who cooperated with *Psyche et Po* for some time, considered feminism as a group of women who seek power and want to be attached to the masculine world. Toril Moi speaks about Cixous's political attitude like this:

Refusal of the label 'feminism' is first and foremost based on a definition of 'feminism' as a bourgeois, egalitarian demand for women to obtain power in the present patriarchal system. Cixous does not reject what she prefers to call the women's movement... and between 1976 and 1982 published all her work with *des femmes* to demonstrate her political commitment to the anti-patriarchal struggle. (Moi 101)

Cixous, by contrast to the power-seeking women, rejects to be a part of the system for the sake of respect or social dignity. She is the first woman who bluntly announced that she is not a feminist (Cited in Moi 101). She believes that the power-seeking feminist critics would trap themselves in the oppressive structure of binary oppositions that is controlled by patriarchal system of thought.

2.3.3. The Reading Strategies of a Text Based on Cixous's Perspectives

The first issue that should be scrutinized when studying a text under each of the various feminist studies including the Cixousian approach is concern for the situations of speech and silence in the female characters. The reasons that could be mentioned for women's experiences of silence are: prohibitions against women's speech and the conventionality of men's speech in contrast to the abnormality of women's speech. Moreover, women's fear of speech and the situations in which women's speech is ignored are among other factors that add to their silence (Eagleton, *Working with Feminist Criticism* 17). Cixous is one of the most significant critics who have cheered women to gain the temerity to break their silences and emancipate their voices. In her "Castration or Decapitation," Cixous writes:

But first she has to speak, start speaking, stop saying that she has nothing to say! Stop learning in school that women are created to listen, to believe, to make no discoveries. Dare to speak her piece about giving, a possibility of a giving that doesn't take away, but gives. Speak of her pleasure and God knows, she has something to say about that, so that she gets to unblock a sexuality that's just as feminine as masculine. . . .

(Cited in Eagleton, *Feminist Literary Theory; A reader* 322)

In the former extract from "Castration or Decapitation?", Cixous delineates her attitudes toward the sexual politics of feminism in addition to encouraging them to speak. She asks women not to block their pleasures of any type but instead provide their development. Furthermore, she insists on the necessity of people's attitudes toward allowing both their feminine and masculine instincts to reside together. Another seminal factor in reading a text from Cixous's perspectives is the characters' and the writer's tendencies to emancipate their voices.

As mentioned in the former sections, culture is constructed in terms of oppositions of good/evil, individual/society and knowledge/ignorance, etc. Hélène Cixous writes, "Thought has always worked through opposition" (Cixous, Clément 63). These oppositions construct the text and are the integral part of ideological concerns. Binary thinking is considered as a means to maintain patriarchy. As a result, critics like Cixous are interested in understanding and dismantling the process of binary thought. Cixous thinks that feminists should challenge the patriarchal binary oppositions especially through deconstructive criticism, since all binary oppositions are "couples" that ends in Man/Woman. In "Sorties," she writes:

Where is she?

Activity/Passivity

Sun/Moon

Culture/Nature

Father/Mother

Head/Emotions

Intelligible/Sensitive

Logos/Pathos.

Form, covex, step, advance, semen, progress.

Matter, concave, ground-where steps are taken, holding- and dumping-ground.

Man____
Woman

   Always the same metaphor: we follow it, it carries us, beneath all its figures, Wherever discourse is organized. If we read or speak, the same thread or double braid is leading us throughout literature, philosophy, criticism, centuries of representation and reflection. Thought has always worked though opposition,

Speaking/Writing

Parole/écriture

High/Low (Cixous, Clément 63).

The aforesaid binary oppositions are continued with "Superior/Inferior, Nature/History, Nature/Art, Nature/Mind, and Passion/Action" (Cixous, Clément *The Newly Born Woman* 64). Cixous notes that the term on the left of the opposition is always privileged and there is "a violent conflict" between both terms as the couple is structured on the repression of the other term (Sarup 110). Without the term on the left of the opposition, the other term becomes meaningless. These binary oppositions do not only operate in the systems of gender and philosophy, but also in the racial and cultural structures of the societies. The structure of power, especially in colonized countries are built on a dualist pair of unequal power. As Mary Eagleton points, they can range from the oppositions such as "Black/White, middle-class/working class, heterosexual/gay to racial dualistic oppositions such as French/Arab, Arab/Jew, and colonizer/colonized" (Eagleton, *Working* 148-50). Cixous writes about the binary oppositions she suffered through racism and anti-Semitism: "So I am three or four years old and the first thing I see in the street is that the world is divided in half, organized hierarchically, and that it maintains this distribution through violence" (Cixous, Clément70). She argues that the world is a hierarchical system which exploits binary oppositions as a form of violence to perpetuate its dominance.

Cixous casts doubt on the unavoidability and naturalness of these systematic hierarchies. She contends to overcome these hierarchies via a strategic and subversive writing practice that is called "feminine writing." One of the features of such a kind of writing is that it does not follow the accepted patterns of writing. It is capable to consist of a series of questions instead of sentences or statements that transfer fixed ideas. During the following extract, she argues about her national identity. It can be viewed how Cixous queries the colonizing hierarchies:

> But I was born in Algeria, and my ancestors lived in Spain, Morocco, Austria, Hungary, Czechoslovakia, Germany; my brothers by birth are Arab. So where are we in history? I side with those who are injured, trespassed upon colonized. I am (not) Arab. Who am I? I am 'doing' French history. I am a Jewish woman. In which ghetto was I penned up during your wars and your revolutions? I want to fight. What is your name? I want to change life. Who is this 'I'? Where is my place? I am looking. I search everywhere. I read, I ask. I begin to speak. Which language is mine? French? German? Arabic? (Cixous, Clément 71)

Cixous denounces the dualistic hierarchies in which the inferior term has to maintain the power and dominance of the superior term over itself. Thus, she aims to unlock these dichotomies because they are oppressing the weaker members within the structure:

There has to be some 'other'- no master without a slave, no economico-political power without exploitation, no dominant class without cattle under the yoke, no 'Frenchmen' without wogs, no Nazis without Jews, no property without exclusion- an exclusion that has its limits and is part of the dialectic. If there were no other, one would invent it. Besides, that is what masters do: they have their slaves made to order. Line for line. They assemble the machine and keep the alternator supplied so that it produces all the oppositions that make economy and thought run. (Cixous. Clément 71)

This paragraph reminds the reader of "Hegel's master/slave relation" (Sarup 110). According to Sarup, Cixous thinks that these "dialectical structures" influence the "formation of subjectivity" (110). In this Hegelian model the subject needs an "Other" from whom he/she can differentiate himself or herself. They not only operate within the racial structures but also in gender structures. In a patriarchal society, woman is always considered as an "Other". She is vital for man's composition and recognition of identity. Under patriarchy, the male is always the victor. Victory is equal to activity and defeat to passivity (Eagleton, *Working* 147). Cixous is at odds with such an equation of passivity with femininity. She tries her best to undo this logocentric ideology, empower a new feminine language and subvert the combination of patriarchal binary schemes, logocentrism and phallocentrism which tries to oppress and silence women. There are other possible oppositions such as intelligible/sensitive, sometimes translated as intelligible/palpable, head/emotions or head/ heart and others that could be diverse in different periods of history (Eagleton, *Working* 147).

Thereupon, it can be assumed that Cixous' ideas and key points about patriarchal binary thought elucidate that the process of thinking is fundamentally binary and the basic opposition for her is male/female. It has been mentioned that binary oppositions cooperate with patriarchal values. As a matter of fact, Cixous aims to dismantle them by creating a subversive language. Moreover, she denounces the equality of femininity with passivity. In her opinion, woman is not passive but on the contrary she is the source of life, power and energy. Cixous is trying to fight the situations that are favored as socially worthwhile by thinkers like Ruskin who aim to domesticate women:

> Woman's voyage: as a body. As if she were destined-in the distribution established by men (separated from the world where cultural exchanges are made and kept in the wings of the social stage when it is a case of History) to be nonsocial, nonpolitical, nonhuman half of the living structure. On nature's side of this structure, of course, tirelessly listening to what goes on inside- inside her belly, inside her 'house'. In direct contrast with her appetites, her affects.
> And, whereas he takes (after the fashion) the risk and responsibility of being an agent, a bit of the public scene where transformations are played out, she represents indifference or resistance to his active tempo; she is the principle of consistency, always somehow the same, everyday and eternal " (Cixous,Clément 66-7).

In her writings, Cixous is creating the open "feminine" and proliferating meaning. This is a way to resist the patriarchal discourse that craves for fixed reproductive identities and fixed meanings resulting from the binary oppositions. Regarding the binary oppositions under the light of Cixous's theories, the ways through which the passage resists them have to be found out. Different aspects of class, race, ethnicity, sexual identity, gender, and also religious difference could be explored under her theories.

The other concepts that could be explored under her theories are "feminine writing" and "feminine reading." On the first stage, it should be made clear what the term "feminine" means in order to investigate the mentioned notions. This is a problematic term of multiple meanings. According to Eagleton, it has almost negative connotations such as "docility, weakness, dependency" in addition to "formlessness, passivity, instability, confinement, piety, materiality, spirituality, irrationality, compliancy, two incorrigible figures: the shrew and the witch" just as been quoted in her *Working with Feminist Criticism* (172). In fact, they are regarded as feminine stereotypes. As a response, some feminists have tried to emphasize the feminine value. They try to celebrate woman's domesticity, mothering, and her female body in general (Eagleton, *Working* 172). The other response toward these stereotypes is to reverse the hierarchies and binary oppositions that have been discussed previously. To put it simply, they try to impose the woman on man, the female to male and the feminine to masculine. The later solution does not seem satisfactory as it can present another form of patriarchy.

According to Moi, the term "feminine" is problematic for English speakers. It is the result of the French word "féminin" (95). In English there are two adjectives for the noun "woman": "female" and "feminine" (Moi 95). According to Moi, whereas "feminine" is used to mention gender as the opposite of "masculine" among Anglo-American feminists, "female" is used to represent sex as a biological feature (95). But in French, the adjective "feminine" conveys both gender and the biological sex. Now the question that is brought up here is that: What does "écriture féminine" mean? Does "feminine writing" refer to something that is based on social constructions of gender? Or is it a text that relies on femaleness?

Another meaning of 'feminine' has been produced in the writings of the French theorists such as Cixous, Irigaray and Kristeva, that is labeled 'feminine writing'. As Eagleton writes, much of the writings of these authors are deeply questioning the construction of knowledge and the play of power within the process of conceptual generation (173). Whereas Kristeva asserts that "woman" is not representable in words, Irigaray defines woman as a "recuperation of the feminine within the logic that maintains it in repression, censorship, nonrecognition" (Cited in Eagleton, *Working*174). Herein, it would be fruitful to understand what the definition of "feminine writing" is in Cixous's terms and point of view. She writes about it in her essay "The Laugh of Medusa," which appeared in the fourth number of the first volume of *Signs*:

> It is impossible to define a feminine practice of writing, and this is an impossibility which will remain, for this practice can never be theorized, enclosed, coded- which doesn't mean that it doesn't exist. But it will always surpass the discourse that regulates the

phallocentric system; it does and will take place in areas other than those subordinated to philosophico theoretical domination. It will be conceived of only by subjects who are breakers of automatisms, by peripheral figures that no authority can ever subjugate. (883)

Indeed, writers and philosophers such as Cixous quest for a meaning of 'feminine' that is not included in the dominant order and exceeds the discourse that is dominant (Eagleton, *Working*173). The 'feminine' is not the era of the controllers, masters and the advocates of the social order but it is the locus for the marginal. It is reserved for the oppressed and the repressed that are not interested in identifying with authority (Eagleton, *Working* 175). Cixous in "The Laugh of Medusa" wishes for those other women especially those who are unacknowledged to talk about their longings that are overflowing and new. She expects the woman to be "ebullient and infinite" (*Signs* Vol.1 No.4 876). She encourages those who dare to sing, to write, to dare to speak and to bring out something new:

> I have been amazed more than once by a description a woman gave me of a world all her own which she had been secretly haunting since early childhood. A world of searching, the elaboration of knowledge, on the basis of asystematic experimentation with the bodily functions, a passionate and precise interrogation of her erotogeneity...Beauty will no longer be forbidden.I wished that woman would write and proclaim this unique empire so that other women, other unacknowledged sovereigns, might exclaim: I, too, overflow; my desire has invented new desires, my body knows unheard-of songs. (*Signs* Vol.1 No.4 875-76)

In fact, the overflowing activity that Cixous talks about includes writing, as well. It is a kind of writing that has a close relation with body and thus is full of pleasure. Cixous also seeks out for laughter as well as song, rhythm, body and metaphor in the text. Such a text touches the reader and helps the woman to return to language and write her femininity. Cixous writes about such writing in her essay "The Laugh of the Medusa," which appears in the fourth number of the first volume of *Signs*:

Text: my body shot through with streams of song; I don't mean the overbearing, clutchy "mother" but, rather, what touches you, the equivoice that affects you, fills your breast with an urge to come to language and launches your force; the rhythm that laughs you; the intimate recipient who makes all metaphors possible and desirable; body (body? bodies?), no more describable than god, the soul, or the Other: that part of you that leaves a space between yourself and urges you to inscribe in language your woman's style. (893)

The waves, floods, outbursts and the fantastic tumult of drives are recognized in a Cixous-like text (Eagleton, *Working* 179). Different parts of writing act like various organs of body. They are connected together and are in motion. There motion results in resistance towards *death*, and death in openness. It should be a lively combination of flying colors, leaves, and rivers within the text that the creators make. The text is like the sea and it is been fed with these elements. In "Castration or Decapitation?" Cixous writes:

Let's not look at the syntax but at the fantasy, at the unconscious: all the feminine texts I've read are very close to the voice, very close to the flesh of language, much more so than the masculine texts... perhaps because they don't rush into meaning, but are straightway at the threshold of feeling. There's tactility in the feminine text, there's touch, and this touch passes through the ear... The innermost touch always echoes in a woman-text. So it is an outpouring... which can appear in primitive or elementary texts as vomiting, as 'throwing up', 'disgorging'. . . .

(Cited in Eagleton, *Working*176)

A seminal aspect of Cixous's writing is that there is no boundary between theoretical writing and creative writing. According to Moi, her style is very metaphorical, anti-theoretical and poetic. There are repetitions of central ideas and images. These elements inspire "non-

59

linear forms of reading" (Moi 101). This kind of writing is meant to stop the divisions between the critical and the creative, the mental and the physical, the poetic and the analytic, the measured and the impassioned, and the formal and the colloquial (Eagleton, *Working*177). In Cixous's writing the meaning is deferred, hence in reading a Cixousian text there is no urge to discover the definite meaning or search for the exact meaning of every line. Another far-reaching feature of a Cixousian feminine writing is that there is no self-censoring. Consequently, when reading a text from the perspectives of Cixous's theories, the researcher should concern with this issue in addition to discovering if there is something that the woman craves to utter but refused to do so. Next, there should be a search for investigating the powerful and creative clues of the secret inner potential in women that is often repressed. The rhythmic qualities, changes in pace, usage of metaphors and puns in a text should be taken under consideration as well (Eagleton, *Working* 177).

There are some elements that should be considered in Cixousian investigation of a text. In the first place, because of her insistence on text as body, it can be assumed that there is a bodily relationship between them. The researcher should have to "work" with the text in Cixous's views. According to Eagleton, she applies the word "work" instead of read (Cited in Eagleton, *Working* 177). This work, according to Cixous, is vocal, graphical and typographical. Listening to the text is a highly momentous factor, as well. And working "typographically," in Cixous's point of view, points to the necessity to consider the text as a body or as a land (Cited in Eagleton, *Working* 179). A scrutiny of its different parts is necessary. As a land, the reader has to look at the trees and rivers of it. In addition, participating in an ongoing and changing process of text's creation; the reading produces certain questions, blind spots, needs and desires is essential. Cixous expresses the existence of a highly physical relation to reading:

I choose to work on the texts that 'touch' me. I use the word deliberately because I believe there is a bodily relationship between reader and text. We work very close to the text, as close to the body of the text was possible; We work phonically, listening to the text, as well as graphically and typographically.

Sometimes I look at the design, the geography of the text, as if it were a map, embodying the world. I look at its legs, its thighs, its belly, as well as its trees and rivers: an immense human and earthly cosmos. I like to work like an ant, crawling the entire length of a text and examining all its details, as well as a bird that flies over it, or one of Tsvetaeva's immense ears, listening to music.

We listen to a text with numerous ears. We hear each other talking with foreign accents, its strangeness, and these acts like signals, attracting our attention. These strangenesses are our cue. We aren't looking for the author as much as what made the author take the particular path they took, write what they wrote. We're looking for the secret of creation each one of us is constantly involved with in the process of our lives. Texts are witnesses of our proceeding. The text opens up a path which is already ours and yet not altogether ours. (Cited in Eagleton, *Working* 180)

There might be some other points about Cixous, her theories as well as feminine writing that the thesis wishes to mention. Cixous believes that woman's difference from man is both biological and linguistic. She aims to present a positive representation of femininity in discourse under the term of "écriture féminine." She believes that the feminine has got the role of 'Other' in the binary oppositions that run in the social script. She declares that the rhetoric of difference that stems from the female body creates new identities for women and finally new social institutions. She also thinks that *jouissance*, which conveys excessive sensual pleasure is operating in the realm of the feminine imaginary. One of the grave facts that have to be mentioned is that feminine writing is not necessarily practiced by a woman but it can be produced by male writers, as well. Jean Genet and James Joyce are the best examples of male writers that practice feminine writing.

Feminine reading and writing are not separate activities and if the researcher wishes to give a short survey of Cixous's ideas about these two concepts, according to Eagleton's *Working with Feminist Criticism* they would be,:

1. Emphasis on the openness

2. Multiple and proliferating meaning

3. "Delighting in 'otherness'"

4. Considering creativity

5. Concern with the body (182)

To summarize, several aspects that are involved in Cixous's theory of feminine writing would be: The questioning of authority, being interested in empowering of the repressed desire over the rational control, attraction to multiplicity for instance multiple identities, exploitation of metaphor and taking an anti-patriarchal as well as anti-sexist position (Eagleton, *Working* 184). These aspects and characteristics seem to be beneficial in the investigation of what Eagleton has listed within the intended texts.

To sum up, what the thesis aims to do throughout the next chapters is to study Zora Neale Hurston's *Their Eyes Were Watching God* and *Seraph on the Suwanee*. Indeed, the researcher is going to pick a number of the listed notions concerning the characteristics of "écriture feminine." One of the selected notions is "emphasis on openness," which according to Briganti and Con Davis is the lack of repressive control in the text (162-4). This notion also includes the ungrammatical structure within the sentences, repetitive words and sentences and circularity of the narration. When a text is open there is no structural order. In addition the text depends on free giving. The other selected notion is multiplicity. A multiple text can be gained by means of metaphors, bisexuality of the author, reader and the characters in addition to the open-endedness of the text. "Concern with physicality and the body," resistance to patriarchy and the "privilege of voice" are the other issues that are going to be applied on the texts based on the theories of Cixous. Although the last notion has not been listed above, Cixous has highly underscored this feature of the feminine writing. To prove this fact, a quotation from her is presented where she writes:

> First I sense femininity in writing by: a privilege of *voice*: *writing* and *voice* are entwined
> and interwoven and writing's continuity/voice's rhythm take each other's breath away
> through interchanging, make the text gasp or form it out of suspenses and silences, make
> it lose its voice or rend it with cries. (Cixous, Clément 92)

To review anew, the researcher has to keep an eye on the selected texts to see if they are capable to bear the notion of 'openness'? Does any emphasis on the 'openness' exist in the author's style of writing? Are any signs of multiplicity and plurality inspected within the texts? In other words, are there any metaphors, puns or is there deferral of meaning? Can any hints and clues to bisexuality be witnessed? Does the passage, the writer or the characters resist authority? Do the texts bear corporeal references? Are they endowed with the boon of voice? Do they contain songs or any other rhythmic qualities? Do the female characters, the marginalized and the oppressed gain voice? These are some of the questions that are going to be answered during the next chapters.

CHAPTER THREE

Words Walking Without Masters

Throughout the following chapters at hand the thesis scrutinizes Zora Neale Hurston's selected novels *Their Eyes Were Watching God* and *Seraph on the Suwanee*. The Cixousian model of feminine writing, which has been discussed heretofore, is applied to the mentioned novels in order to find out whether they are capable to be considered as écriture féminine. The aforesaid elements of openness, multiplicity, body, otherness, voice as well as the factors of creativity and resisting patriarchy are the fundamental characteristics of a feminine writing. This research determines to deal with the concepts of body, multiplicity, openness and voice as well as the issue of dismantling patriarchy.

Henceforth, the thesis deals with the investigation of a selected number of the mentioned notions within the texts of *Their Eyes Were Watching God* and *Seraph on the Suwanee*. Moreover, the excerpts that elucidate these notions are presented to the readers. The thesis tries to compare the exemplifications with Cixous's assertions, stated in her theoretical and poetical essays. Prior to the inauguration of this study, it might be beneficial to encompass a brief summary of the novels in order to develop a more tangible understanding of the related quotations and paraphrases.

According to the text of the novel, *Their Eyes Were Watching God* is the story of a beautiful African-American woman with the blood of the whites in her vessels as both her grandmother and mother were sexually assaulted by white men. Janie, the heroine of the story is the result of a white teacher assaulting her young mother after one school day. Right in the second chapter of the novel the readers learn that she is brought up by her grandmother, Nanny. One day that Janie is sitting under a blooming pear tree in spring, she envisions marriage after watching the bees and blooms along with the coupling flies in the kitchen.

Hereby, she longs for a bee to fulfill her passionate dreams. Nanny finds out that Janie's womanhood is awakening when she watches out Janie letting Johnny Taylor kissing her; hence she makes her marry brother Logan Killicks.

It does not take Janie a long time to understand that marriage does not necessarily inhere in love. In chapter three of the novel, the readers recognize that upon Logan's coercing her to work on the field, Janie decides to elope with Joe Starks after getting acquainted with him. Joe reminds her of the horizon, but he is not the incarnation of the bee revolving around the blossoms. Although she is aware of the mentioned fact, she is still hopeful. Joe Starks silences Janie and prohibits her from speaking in public because he believes that women are not made for this purpose. Moreover, he forces Janie to wear a head rag in the store as he is jealous of people's recognition of his wife's beautiful hair and tries to circumscribe it. Janie endures him for nearly twenty years until she sees no other way than to rebel against him. Consequently, Joe becomes badly sick and Janie gets emancipated by his death. Thereupon, she burns all her head rags and sits on the porch in the evenings to listen to stories.

At last Tea Cake; the bee of her blossom, appears in her life and in the story. They develop a romantic relationship and despite the wealthy suitors' offers, the community's gossips and their warnings, Janie marries him. They leave Eatonville for Jacksonville and then the Everglades where they go to work on the fields with workers. Tea Cake and Janie do not live together for a long time. They are trapped in the hurricane, which forces them to leave the Everglades for the Palm Beach. In the way, Tea Cake is attacked by a rabid dog while he is trying to save Janie from it. He gets absolutely insane after nearly three weeks and attempts to kill Janie by his pistol. Janie, struggling for her life, shoots him with the rifle a little bit sooner than his shot to secure herself.

On the other hand, *Seraph on the Suwanee,* according to the author of the story, is about the white Arvay. She is marginal in the sense that she is a Cracker, therefore she belongs to the lower strata of society. She suffers from hysterical spasms until she gets married. Her husband Jim wins her by applying two violent actions of spilling turpentine in her eye followed with an attack, since he can bind her to himself in no other way. They cannot get on very well in their marriage as a consequence of their inability to have a successful dialogue or communication with each other. In addition, Earl, their first child is a mentally handicapped son who obsesses Arvay's mind very successively even after he dies. It is through her second abandonment of her marital life that she reaches a good understanding of her self, her life and her family, particularly her husband. This recent empowerment helps her to return home and go on board to meet Jim more confidently hereupon. She becomes successful in revealing her mind and her concealed power to Jim.

Heretofore, brief summaries of the selected novels are presented. Thus, the thesis is going to deal with the notion of plurality, which is a significant concept of feminine writing, in the next discussion. This raised issue relates to the linguistic quality of a text.

3.1. Plural Expressions, Plural Identities

Metaphor is a figure of speech which describes one item in the form of another. One of the serious tools to achieve plurality or multiplicity in writing is metaphor. They are impressive tropes of language by means of which, figurative statements, depth, multiplicity and plurality of meanings are produced from simple words and phrases. Multiplicity of meanings is a sign of a deconstructive text, mainly a Derridean as well as a Cixousian one. Therefore, one of the characteristics of a feminine writing is multiplicity. In this section, the researcher tries to reveal the multiplicity of the selected texts by offering a number of the metaphoric phrases and their connotations.

One of the most notable stylistic devices that Hurston uses within both of the novels, are metaphors. She creates her female characters by means of the extensive use of metaphors to convey their growth into strong self-assured and independent individuals after overcoming the various gender roles that are imposed on them. Not only in *Their Eyes* but also in *Seraph*, metaphors perform significant roles in enhancing the reader's understanding of key issues throughout the story. Hurston occupies the reader's mind with outstanding comparisons. If some of these metaphors are overlooked, major understandings produced by means of the proliferated meanings are condemned to be missed.

One of the most primary metaphors in *Their Eyes Were Watching God*, according to Wolfgram is the metaphor of the sea, which emerges the very first ("Literary Device Evaluation"). On the surface, the readers see the sea with its tides, waves and the ships. Indeed, Hurston applies the metaphor of the sea to claim that the longings of different types of men differ. Furthermore, the metaphor of the sea reveals how different women are from men in respect of their dreams:

> Ships at a distance have every man's wish on board. For some they come in with the tide. For others they sail forever on the horizon, never out of sight, never landing until the Watcher turns his eyes away in resignation, his dreams mocked to death by Time. That is the life of men.
>
> Now, women forget all those things they don't want to remember and remember everything they don't want to forget. The dream is the truth. Then they act and do things accordingly. (Hurston, *Their Eyes* 1)

This metaphor manifests its domination throughout the entire book. Joe Starks is the latter type of man. He is highly ambitious and always strives for more. As he gets older, he particularly realizes to what extent his dreams are "mocked to death by Time" (Hurston, *Their Eyes* 1). He is not in a good shape as he used to be; besides he is confronted with many problems even with sitting down on a chair (Hurston, *Their Eyes* 77). As a result of his excessive pride, Joe cannot concede that he needs to consult with a doctor (Hurston, *Their Eyes* 83). Henceforward, he undergoes a premature demise. It can be assumed that he has finally "turned his eyes away in resignation." In contrast with Joe Starks, Tea Cake is of the other type of man. He is content with his life, wife, wealth and jobs. Thus, his dreams had "come in with the tide" (Hurston, *Their Eyes* 1).

Hurston defines women plainly in the aforementioned metaphor. Janie reveals the signs of what her dream is and what she remembers. By marrying Logan "Janie's first dream is dead, so she became a woman" (Hurston, *Their Eyes* 30). The postponement of her dream paves the way for her maturity. All she longs throughout her life is a true mutual love, which she achieves by marrying Tea Cake. The next objective that she has certainly thirst for is freedom. The evidence of how women remember is most brightly recognized when Janie returns to Eatonville after Tea Cake's death. She recalls her good moments with Tea Cake and his memories, not her other husbands, because she perceives Tea Cake as still living (Hurston, *Their Eyes* 193). She determines what she wants to remember and what she does not want to remember. Janie's attitude toward her past springs Cixous's proclamation of past and its effect on future to the minds. In "The Laugh of the Medusa" she states: "The future must no longer be determined by the past. I do not deny that the effects of the past are still with us. But I refuse to strengthen them by repeating them...." (*Signs* Vol.1, No.4 875) The bitter memories of the past are barred from entering her present life. Comparing Cixous's statement, Janie is different in the point that she meditates on the present. Janie does not "confer upon" her past in order to submit them as the determiners of her present and future life (*Signs* Vol.1, No.4 875). Janie recounts them to Phoeby to prove her development into a free woman who is proficient in the art of storytelling.

The most recurring metaphor, in Haurykiewics's view, that is dominant in the first half of the novel is that of the mule (45). It is recognized to its full extent in Nanny's comparison of woman to it. Janie's grandmother declares: "De nigger woman is de mule uh de world so fur as Ah can see" (Hurston, *Their Eyes* 14). The "mule" is considered as the representative of the oppressed and repressed subjects. This is the reason why Janie sympathizes with Matt

69

Bonner's mule and loathes people abusing "helpless things" (Hurston, *Their Eyes* 67). In spite of what Nanny wishes for her grandchild, she is converted to "mule" due to her husbands' efforts to dominate, exploit and rule her in their own manners. According to Beneš, Hurston, however, transgresses the metaphor of the mule by letting the oppressed woman revolt against her master and urging her to kill him whether by disclosing the bitter truth of their marital life or in the form of self-defense (6). Another connotation of mule is silence. As Haurykiewicz argues, Janie journeys the pathway from the level of a mule to the level of what she terms "muliebrity" (45). She states that, "muliebrity" is defined as "the state or condition of being a woman" by the OED (Cited in Haurykiewics 45), hence it conveys the state of being a woman who possesses "full womanly powers" (Haurykiewics 45). Haurkiewicz believes that Hurston's purpose is to illuminate the difference between silence and speech as well as its effect on Janie's life. Moreover, the image of mule in *Their Eyes*, embodies a "potential resistance to the status quo" (Haurkiewicks, 47) in addition to being "a beast of burden" (Haurkiewicks 46-7). Thus, Janie is transformed from a silent worker and wife to an empowered as well as a free woman by means of practicing the obstinate manners of a trickster mule. In his way, it is presumed that the metaphor of the mule is adapted to point to different sides of Janie's personality, her development and her marriages.

Another similar threatening vision that frightens Nanny of Janie's future is unfolded through the metaphor of "spittoon" or the "spit cup" (Hurston, *Their Eyes* 20). She warns Janie: "And Ah can't die easy thinkin' maybe de menfolks white or black is makin' a spit cup outa you: Have some sympathy fuh me. Put me down easy, Janie, Ah'm a cracked plate" (Hurston, *Their Eyes* 20). This metaphor can convey sexual harassment. Nanny is worried about Janie being lacerated and abused by men as happened to herself and her daughter Leafy. Janie suffers from sexual exploitation, notwithstanding she marries, as all her three husbands seek to dominate her body by dint of their patriarchal deeds. Logan attempts to make "a beast

70

of burden" out of Janie (Haurkiewicz 54), while Joe Starks sets her on "a pedestal" and tries to make a "wife" out of her (Hurston, *Their Eyes* 29). Tea Cake can be blamed for his possessive attitudes toward Janie and his attempt to beat her in order to prove others that he is her boss (Hurston, *Their Eyes* 148). The researcher is intellectually congruent with McGlamery who argues that Nanny's vision of spittoon is verified, since in addition to the porch sitters who judge Janie and "have her up in their mouths," Jody puts air on other people via Janie alongside his magnificent golden spit cup (111-12). Therefore, she is considered as a means of maintaining Jody's power. Janie's arm is another locus of the metaphor of spittoon as Tea Cake "dies salivating" on it, when he closes "his teeth in the flesh of her forearm" (McGlamery 112; Hurston184).

Other noteworthy metaphors, according to Lund and Wolfgram are the metaphors of "horizon," "pear tree" and "hurricane" ("Metaphors in *Their Eyes Were Watching God*"; "Literary Device Evaluation"). The metaphor of "horizon" is exposed initially "with an ode to Horizon" that appears in the very first paragraph where readers observe those "[s]hips at a distance" with "every man's wish on the board" that "sail forever on the horizon, never out of sight, never landing until the Watcher turns his eyes in resignation ..." (King 54; Hurston, *Their Eyes* 1). Herein, the image of horizon seems to suggest the ultimate and the extreme limit of fulfillment of man's dreams. The presence of words such as "distance", "sight", "Watcher", and "eyes" offers a further connotation. It conveys vision and a possibility for gaze. These concepts are spread throughout the novel from the very beginning to the end. The first incarnation of the mentioned concepts is the title of the story, *Their Eyes Were Watching God*. It suggests that the capability of gaze is ascertained for a number of people including Janie, the protagonist, who is deprived of it in spite of being its object. In addition, the horizon plays a role at "sundown" when the porch sitters sit "in judgment" at the end of a labor day and as Daram and Hozhabrsadat argue, fail to seek for the horizon, quite unlike Janie that is "an individual who strives for the horizon" (87). Joe Starks is considered as another embodiment of horizon throughout the novel. Janie's intuition of this man illustrates that "he did not represent sun-up and pollen and blooming trees, but he spoke for far horizon. He spoke for change and chance" (Hurston, *Their Eyes* 29). King supports the narrator's definition of horizon by stating that Jody represents "possibility" (55). Janie is a victim of Logan's impotency, scurrilous remarks, and his failure in listening to Janie's words as well as his attempts to push her into coerced labor. As a consequence, the seventeen-year-old Janie is forced to elope with Jody who wants "to be a big voice", and speaks "for far horizon" (Hurston, *Their Eyes* 28-9). Janie wants to make a trip to the horizon, and her journey becomes a principal metaphor in the story. Furthermore, horizon is the final destination of Janie's lifelong journey to achieve self-actualization and self-revelation. Janie does not embrace her self-fulfillment unless she links herself to her community. Thus, from the perspective of Kubitsechek, "the novel strongly implies communal enjoyment of, and benefit from, the quester's prize" (109). This prize includes Janie's experience of self-integrity as well as her "hard won knowledge" (Kubitschek 109). At the end of the novel Janie utters: "Ah done been tuh de horizon and back and now. Ah kin set heah in mah house and live by comparison" (191). Janie embarks on her quest in order to discover a new definition of her self, which is different from her former subjectivities that have been formed from patriarchal notions. Therefore, as Kubitschek puts forth, Janie sets out for "a female quest" (109). Another view is put forward according to what Hemenway suggests as "the horizon motif" (Cited in Lee 114). Derived from his conception, the "horizon motif," elucidates the distance that has to be passed in order to discriminate between "illusion and reality, dream and truth, role and self" (Cited in Lee 114). Janie is not able to discern between these issues until she embarks on her journey "to show her shine" (Hurston, *Their Eyes* 90). The last connotation of the metaphor of horizon that is presented in this part is proposed by Patrick S. Bernard. Janie

72

disparages Nanny of taking "the biggest thing God ever made, the horizon---for no matter how far a person can go, the horizon is still way beyond you---and pinched it in to such a little bit of a thing that she could tie it about her grandmother's neck tight enough to choke her" (Hurston, *Their Eyes* 89). Herein, the mind is conceptualized as "an abstract thing though in sensual as well as physical terms." Thereupon, the terms "to choke" and to "twist" as well as the phrase "biggest thing God has ever made---the horizon," implies the suffocation of mind (Bernard 10). As Bernard persuasively argues:

> To Janie the mind, or its metaphor the horizon, is the collective aspects of her intellect and consciousness. It is the sum total of her mental powers, including how she understands, conceives, judges, reasons, thinks, wills, desires, and chooses. But the mind also anchors her memory and remembrance. By the mind, we understand how she thinks and speaks to herself and us. (Bernard 10)

As a consequence, horizon can also covey Janie's mind and mentality. From the mentioned arguments as well as quotations, it can be assumed that the metaphor of horizon seems to offer a multitude of connotations, hence a multi-layered meaning, which results in plurality of meanings that is derived from this concept. In addition to plurality, this concept may establish another connection to femininity, via its introduction of the notion of female quest for self-discovery, since it creates a female bond between women.

The most powerful metaphor in *Their Eyes* is perhaps the metaphor of the pear tree. Janie is enchanted by the beautiful blossoming pear tree in Nanny's backyard. Janie intuits the meaning of true love when she observes the marriage of the bees to the blossoms of the pear tree. The blossoming pear tree symbolizes Janie's emerging womanhood and flourishing libido. Janie's image of love, as she perceives from the pear tree, motivates her to embark on her lifelong search for love. The image of the pear tree is in the background of any decision that she makes regarding love and marriage. She compares her suitors with this image. It is only Tea Cake who proves to be a bee for her blossom. Janie perceives Tea Cake as the

73

embodiment of the penetrating bees. By marrying him, she reaches to sensual fulfillment and achieves self-realization thereafter.

Hurston applies metaphors to help the readers see what Janie is discovering in her life with Joe Starks. The following paragraphs do not only express Janie's discoveries but also men's attitudes toward women in marriage:

> The spirit of marriage left the bedroom and took to living in the parlor. It was there to shake hands whenever company came to visit, but it never went back inside the room again. So she put something in there to represent the spirit like a Virgin Mary image in a church. The bed was no longer a daisy-field for her and Joe to play in. It was a place where she went and laid down when she was sleepy and tired.
> She stood there until something fell off the shelf inside her. Then she went inside there to see what it was. It was her image of Jody tumbled down and shattered. But looking at it she saw that it never was the flesh and blood figure of her dreams. Just something she had grabbed up to throw her dreams over."
>
> (Hurston, *Their Eyes* 72)

As the later passage illustrates, Janie is convinced that their marriage is not amicable and Jody does not represent her dreams. Hence, her dreams are "shattered" (Hurston, *Their Eyes* 72). By representing Joe as a fragile ornament that falls from a shelf, Hurston fulfills the idea of pedestal by locating Jody (Joe Starks) on it so that he is not capable of being matched with Janie's expectations. Thus, she can recognize "no more blossomy openings" over Jody (72). These paragraphs bear two further metaphors, as well. The image of "Virgin Mary" and the idea of "the bed" not representing "daisy-field" points to Janie's lack of sensual fulfillment as well as their marriage's shortcomings in offering wedded bliss.

Yet again Hurston shows her mastery in the art of figurative language by presenting how an individual possesses a special capacity to show one's self. This metaphor reveals how each person is endowed with an inner special boon that shines, though it is often buried under "mud" and is not able to glimmer. Janie is not allowed to shine and exposes her true self until the death of Joe and the appearance of Tea cake because she is covered up by oppressive circumscriptions. The application of this metaphor shows the fact that Tea Cake and Janie can find each other and be who they truly are. Hurston writes about Janie and Tea Cake's inner capacity in this way:

> When God had made The Man, he made him out of stuff that sung all the time and glittered all over. Then after that some angels got jealous and chopped him into millions of pieces, but still he glittered and hummed. So they beat him down to nothing but sparks but each little spark had a shine and a song. So they covered each one over with mud. And the lonesomeness in the sparks make them hunt for another, but the mud is deaf and dumb. Like the other tumbling mud-balls, Janie had tried to show her shine. (Hurston, *Their Eyes* 90)

The last sentence of this recent quotation is very impressive and influential in the researcher's point of view. It is an evidence of Janie's thirst for realizing her identity as well as her attempt to discover her own values aside from the conventional principles.

Janie's beautiful hair could be considered as another influential metaphor in the novel. Janie's abundant long black hair seems to be her prettiest corporeal endowment that receives noteworthy emphasis throughout the story. Being an indicative sign of her femininity, it is both praised and abused. In addition to being an object of gaze, it becomes a site of Jody's oppression, since he orders her to wear a head rag because of being jealous of others wondering over it. After his death, Janie burns all of her head rags in a symbolic act of emancipation. The community recognizes "the only change" after Jody's death, as a consequence her hair transfers into a site of resistance. When she returns to Eatonville, the male community notices it as "a great rope of black hair swinging to her waist and unraveling in the wind like a plume" (Hurston, *Their Eyes* 2). Herein, her hair becomes an object of gaze, as "the men, were saving with the mind what they lost with the eye", as a result of their attitudes, it obtains an oppressive role (Hurston, *Their Eyes* 2).

In chapter twelve, Phoeby goes to meet Janie in order to convince her to marry the entrepreneur who is from Sanford in addition to getting some information about her relationship with Tea Cake. But Janie has already made her decision to marry Tea Cake stealthily. Therefore, she tells Janie: "We'se just good as married already. But Ah ain't puttin' it in de street. Ah'm tellin' *you*" (Hurston, *Their Eyes* 114). Phoeby reacts: "Ah jus lak uh chicken. Chicken drink water, but he don't pee-pee" (114). According to Gale Cengage whose discussion has appeared in enotes webpage, the metaphor of the "chicken" is another metaphor within *Their Eyes*. Just like a little chicken that does not urinate after drinking water in front of people, Phoeby promises Janie to keep her plan secret. It reveals the truthfulness, steadfastness and fidelity of the listener.

The strategic sentence, "Their Eyes Were Watching God," which appears in the eighteenth chapter and is the title of *Their Eyes*, would be a further metaphor to be mentioned and discussed here (160). On the previous page of the novel, this sentence appears in another similar way: "Six eyes were questioning God" (159). It reveals that they are questioning God throughout the hurricane and the attack of the cruel wind. The passage that includes this remarkable statement is: "They sat in company with the others in other shanties, their eyes straining against crude walls and their souls asking if he meant to measure their puny might against His. They seemed to be staring at the dark, but their eyes were watching God" (160). It conveys a sense of fate and destiny. Tea Cake and Janie feel the control of a higher power that has their lives in his fist. It also indicates their beliefs in the presence of God. In addition, it conveys that the watchers expect God's help and the opportunity of a longer life. The last connotation that is going to be mentioned in this section is the capability of gaze that is concealed within the title of the book. The three people who are gazing at God, the transcendental signified and the ultimate logocentric truth, have been marginalized and the objects of the oppressors' gaze all through their lives because of being black and in Janie's

76

case, being a black woman. If gaze is considered as a competence that powerful subjects possess, it is taken for granted that the hierarchical relation is reversed in this situation, as these are the marginalized subjects who gaze at the ultimate authority.

Janie's childhood name reveals an existent multiplicity within her. During Janie's childhood, everybody used to call her by a different name. Understanding that she possesses multiple names, others decide to call her "Alphabet" (Hurston, *Their Eyes* 9). "Alphabet" offers plurality of names, and as names are signs of identity, it is competent to convey plural identities. When Janie narrates her story to Phoeby, she says the reason she was called "Alphabet" is that everybody called her with different names. Janie's marginalization could be regarded as the main reason of her different names as well as plural identities. She is neither black nor white by birth. In addition, she is grown up in the white people's dwelling and wears their clothes despite belonging to the black community. Thus, as a child she recognizes herself in the picture shown to her. When she inspects it carefully, she recognizes her dress and her hair, then utters shockingly: "'Aw, aw! Ah'm colored!'" (Hurston, *Their Eyes* 9). It can be assumed that, in the beginning, she realizes her identity through comparison with the White culture. When she becomes a mature woman she actualizes herself via Nanny's, Logan's and Joe Starks's values who are the representatives of the conventional male-regulated culture. Later, she protests against these conventions by marrying Tea Cake and keeps on resisting other patriarchal notions thereafter. In this way, she achieves fulfillment and understands her subjectivity. Some Hurston scholars believe that Janie's identity becomes actualized through her return to her racial roots. For instance, Mary Helen Washington approves of "Janie's search for identity and her connections to her community" (Cited in Walker 3). The process of Janie's identity development undoubtedly approaches to its integrity just when she stops her silence and rises up her voice against her oppressors. Janie's improvement in adaptation of language which is exposed through her art of wordplay and storytelling has to be considered as influential factors in the formation of her subjectivity. As Kubitschek convincingly argues, "Janie, always sufficiently knowledgeable of the white culture, to ensure her survival, discover her own soul only through the art of storytelling..." (109). The other notable point is that Janie's subjectivity is in process. She develops different subjectivities that are defined either by others or by her own self. She never achieves a unified self, due to the multiple subjectivities reside within her.

As it was mentioned previously, there are various metaphors in *Seraph on the Suwanee*, as well. A number of metaphors seem to be common in both of the selected texts. The metaphor of the mule is also present in *Seraph on the Suwanee* though in the form of "horse". Frustrated by Arvay's contradictory behavior, Jim seeks for remedy from Joe Kelsey. His advice is nothing but to tackle her like a horse or in its broader connotation, captivate her like a mule, when he suggests: "Most women folks will love you plenty if you take and see to it that they do. Make 'em knuckle under. From the very first jump, get the bridle in their mouth and ride 'em hard and stop 'em short. They's all alike, Boss, Take 'em and break 'em" (Hurston, *Seraph* 46). According to Beneš, after a painful internal struggle, Arvay revolts against her master finally to prove him her power and becomes successful in gaining his respect. By means of this metaphor, Hurston approaches with a new imagery for the new, aware and liberated black woman (6).

The pear tree of *Their Eyes Were Watching God* is substituted with the mulberry tree in *Seraph on the Suwanee* although Arvay does not justify her husband with her tree as Janie does. As Morris and Dunn argue, the mulberry tree turns to "Arvay's image of herself" (Cited in Jones 159). The mulberry tree helps Arvay to reach self-revelation and consequently discover her latent sensual and reproductive power. The mulberry tree is exhibited four times throughout the novel.

The first time, Arvay takes Jim to the garden and shows it to him as a reminder of her childhood playhouse. Here, the mulberry tree is a symbol of Arvay's naivety. In addition to being her playhouse, it is considered as a "sacred place" as it was once the site of meditating on her first love, Carl (Hurston, *Seraph* 37). But now, she wishes her territory to be "cleansed" from the memory of Carl and locates Jim instead of him (Hurston, *Seraph* 37).

The second time that readers are faced with the scene of the mulberry tree is when Jim seduces Janie by inflicting a premature intimacy on her in order to bind her to himself. In this place it becomes the symbol of Arvay's experience along with being a site of her exploitation and enslavement. According to Morris and Dunn, the tree represents a new meaning to Arvay. When she puts her underwear on one of its branches it becomes "a symbol of loss of innocence and virginity" (Cited in Jones 159).

The third time that Arvay goes to see the tree she reviews the memory of the mentioned affair. Upon sitting under the tree, she realizes that she has been a slave to that man" (Hurston, *Seraph* 134)! Hence, she admits her enslavement. However, she convinces herself to return to her marital residence not for Jim's sake but to free herself from her parents' ugly poor house (Hurston, *Seraph* 135). The last time that she sits under the mulberry tree is when she has just finished burning her inherited old cracked house nearly the end of the novel. This time she experiences a new feeling, she feels "exultation," since "It is the first time in her life that she is conscious of feeling that way. She had always felt like an imperfect ball restlessly bumping and rolling and rolling and bumping. Now she feels that she has to come to a dead and absolute rest" (Hurston 307). Herein, the mulberry tree bears the significance of Arvay's freedom. Beneš thinks that by applying this powerful imagery that connects characters to natural elements such as specific trees, in addition to her adaptation of the mule metaphor which exemplifies the transformation from repression to management of one's life, Hurston provides a distinct portrayal of oppressed women, by emphasizing their bodies, expressing their longings, and their search for the self (9). According to the mentioned arguments, it is presumed that the mulberry tree is a significant metaphor that produces multiple layers of meaning within the novel. It is fruitful to point to the commonality of the substantial presence of natural elements in both Hurston's and Cixous's works. In one of her influential essay, Cixous asserts that: "Often I go read in a tree. Far from the ground and the shit. Idon't go paradise. I am searching: somewhere there must be people who are like me in their rebellion and in their hope" (Cixous, Clément 72). Similar to Cixous, Janie and Arvay; the heroines of the stories go toward their trees to read their identities, write their dreams and meditate on their subjectivities. They seek refuge in their trees and commence their searches for fulfillment and rebellion against repressions from there.

Expressions such as "brash devil" (Hurston 8) or "Devil's doll-baby" (Hurston 15) are considered as metaphors. They are used by the author to portray Jim's personality in *Seraph on the Suwanee*. In spite of his good characteristics, Jim has an excessive chauvinism that leads Arvay to experience the hell to live with him. When Arvay is worried about her young girl's "taking company," she remembers her own marriage and concentrates on it. Her discoveries are revealed through very impressive metaphoric sentences:

> For a space, Arvay traveled the road that she had come for the last twenty years. Her love had mounted her to the tops of peaky mountains. It had dragged her the dust. She had been in Hell's kitchen and licked all the pots. She had stood for moments on the right side of God. (Hurston, *Seraph* 176)

These lines along with the metaphors that describe Jim have further connotations, as well. They have interconnectedness with Arvay's spiritual devotion to missionary service. Jim scorned the idea that Arvay is hopeless with the world and is not concerned with love (Hurston, *Seraph* 8). He courts Arvay until he makes her succumb to their marriage.

Consequently, Arvay could not follow the missionary anymore, as she is a married woman then. She continues to have a deep faith in Christianity though.

The other metaphor is revealed in the name of the boats. During the last years that Jim goes after the shrimp business Arvay never visits the port until she makes her decision about reunion with Jim. There she sees that his boats are named after the members of her family, one of which is *Arvay Henson*. It is noteworthy that Jim used Arvay's paternal last name and not his own refer to her. The maintenance of a woman's paternal family name even after her marriage could be an indicative of her possession of identity, hence it bears feminist hints.

The final scenes of *Seraph on the Suwanee* are capable to remind the reader of the prologue in *Their Eyes Were Watching God* where "[s]hips at a distance have dreams of every man's wish on board" (1). As Beneš states, "Hurston extends the metaphor here in a powerful episode on the sea, where Jim and Arvay reunite" (102). This similarity of metaphor results in depth of the story. As Jim is steering the wheel of *Arvay Henson* through the havoc "with her mouth wide open," the readers remind the hurricane in *Their Eyes Were Watching God* (Hurston, *Seraph* 328). When they overcome the havoc, a new horizon appears for Arvay: "The contrast was utterly startling. No waves, just an undulating motion that made the distant horizon seem to go up and down slowly and gently" (Hurston, *Seraph* 330). The stormy sea and the calmness followed by the storm is a metaphoric point to foreshadow Arvay and Jim's married life in future. They had a stormy life as a result of Arvay's repression and Jim's misunderstanding. But they reunite eventually and recommence a peaceful life as Arvay gains self-confidence and self-revelation. In addition to the sea, the horizon performs a notable role within *Seraph* similar to *Their Eyes*. In both of the novels, the sea signifies the location of dreams. They can be devastated or fulfilled there. Quite like Janie, Arvay goes on a processed search for self-discovery. She travels different stages throughout her life in order to achieve self-revelation and peace of mind and meets the horizon thereafter. The horizon could be regarded as the ultimate peacefulness in the mentioned quotation. Jim and Arvay keep on their conversation about the sea. Arvay expresses her feeling of belonging: "Seems like I been off somewhere on a journey and just got home." Jim admits her by saying: "Once I had seen and been on the sea, it got inside me, and I ever longed for it like a drop of water" (Hurston, *Seraph* 333). The sea is the metaphor of Arvay's self that was fragmented but has recently gained its strength and commences its reunion. Jim declares that the drops of water "runs into a bigger river and all that millions-times multiplied drops of water marches like an army back to the sea" (333). Arvay assures him that "it will return to its real self at last" (334). Indeed, she refers to her fragmented self that approaches its reunion. The aforementioned metaphor is another means of exposing the idea of "subject in process" and plural subjectivities.

The scenes that portray the sea are also capable to represent it as a new space where Arvay is able to reunite with Jim. As pointed out before, Hurston goes on extending and working with the sea metaphor into new levels, here. The conversation about the sea and its origins can refer to their shared journey through the twenty years of marriage. Jim tells her that:

> The very same water that you see out there was right here when the world was formed. Changed places and forms too many thousands of times for you to imagine, been off from home and come back just that many times. I look at it and think about it, and I never get tired of looking and thinking. (Hurston, *Seraph* 334)

Jim is talking about Arvay, through metaphors. Hurston connects Arvay's color of eyes to the sea as well as her journey from a poor Cracker to the queen via Jim's words. It reveals Jim's fascination with both Arvay and the sea, and reminds the reader of the enigma that Arvay's eyes are to Jim. It explains Jim's moody behavior towards Arvay and their fights: "the sea never gives in; it is an ever-moving force in need of taming if one wishes to stay alive"

82

(Hurston, *Seraph* 334). As Jones persuasively argues, Hurston adapts natural elements such as the sea "as a means of testing the relationship between Jim and Arvay" (159). She continues by asserting that their marriage is saved by means of reconciliation of their differences (160). Moreover, the quoted passages convey a sense of stubbornness as well as empowerment. They are competent to reveal that Arvay is too obstinate and powerful to submit since she views "power and freedom in the sea" (160). Therefore, Jim has to tame Arvay in order to "stay alive." Beneš states that: "the sea can both kill, like Arvay tried earlier, and provide spectacles such as Arvay's beautiful eyes and her devoted love for Jim" (102). Reading the metaphor in this way leads to assume that Arvay understands what Jim is saying by uttering: "Maybe it's like with everything and everybody. If it's there, it will return to its real self at last" (Hurston, *Seraph* 334). She is revealing her attempts to approach integrity and embrace self-realization.

According to Tate, a further literary device that produces layers of meaning in *Seraph on the Suwanee* is pun (Cited in Bloom 147). Pun is a significant trope to proliferate meanings within a text. According to Tate, there are two layers of meaning in *Seraph on the Suwanee*. If it is read under the light of the psychoanalytic approach, it would turn out to be a "subversive and parodic joke," as stated by Tate, through observing the existing racial and sexual codes and their different related literal meanings. The text contains "metahumorous carnivalsque discourses" that result in double production along with a capability of combination (Cited in Bloom 151). They are influential in producing humor and parody, thus Hurston adapts them to proclaim her disagreement with the accepted social relationships between different races and sexes.

There are other means of proliferating meanings in *Seraph on the Suwanee*. "I can read your writing" is a sentence uttered by both Arvay and Jim subsequently. It demonstrates the uncovered desires within the text. As Tate points, it reveals not only Jim's discovery of

83

Arvay's desires being concealed under a heavy pile of repressions, but also Arvay's understanding of what Jim genuinely longs in spite of applying banters and controlling behavior (Cited in Bloom 151). The text of *Seraph on the Suwanee* is not as transparent as its characters' behaviors. In a psychoanalytic reading of the novel, the meaning can be interpreted not only by reading the conscious explicit dialogue, but also can be decoded by the unconscious discourses of desire. Meaning is deferred in *Seraph on the Suwanee* and thus is not revealed simply.

Another means of producing plurality is bisexuality. Bisexuality is the multiplicity of beings. It is a sign of plurality in a Cixousian text. As Cixous writes, bisexuality is "a fantasy of a complete being, which replaces the fear of castration" (Cixous, Clément 84). Bisexuality is a site where both sexes are present. As a result, the effects of desire's inscription on every part of the body and the other body are multiplied (Cixous, Clément 85). Bisexuality is almost connected to femininity, since a woman, unlike man, does not repress the other biological identity within herself as a man does.

One of the most metaphoric sentences in *Their Eyes Were Watching God* appears in chapter one. Janie tells Phoeby Watson: "You can tell 'em what Ah say if you wants to. Dat's just de same as me 'cause mah tongue is in mah friend's mouf" (6). On the surface as well as within the context of the story, it means that Phoeby is Janie's delegate in their community. She can tell what she has been told in order to defend Janie. Hurston has included a hidden homoerotic longing in the unconscious of this text. This is a reference to the presence of both male and female desires and therefore bisexuality within the text as well as Janie and Phoeby. Similar to Janie's tongue, Phoeby's "hungry listening" is a sign of "female generativity" within the text of *Their Eyes* (Hurston 10; McGlamery 122). It is next to impossible for Janie to narrate her story in "soft, easy phrases" without Phoeby's listening. The aforementioned statement as well as phrase can suggest that Janie fulfills her reproductive and generative potentials by means of storytelling.

Another evidence of the existence of bisexuality could be Janie's wearing overalls. In spite of wearing jeans which were typical of men in those times, she wore them without her femininity being distorted. Consequently, her friend confesses that: "Even wid dem overhalls on, you shows yo' womanhood" (Hurston, *Their Eyes* 4).

Phoeby and Janie have been "kissin' –friends" for about twenty years (Hurston, *Their Eyes Were Watching God* 7). It is also mentioned that they have been "bosom friends" (114). These phrases point to the close friendship between Janie and Phoeby. But on a deeper level it contains an erotic quality that adds to the bisexual nature of the text in addition to Janie and Phoeby's relationship.

Arvay's bisexuality is displayed in an aggressive manner on the other hand. She is very curious about her sister Larraine's pregnancy and matrimony (Hurston, *Seraph* 12). The narrator reveals Arvay's interest in being in her sister's bedroom and spying everything that is going on there. Arvay detests her sister to death because she has been always preferred over Arvay. She also marries Carl whom Arvay loves. Now that Arvay is married to Jim in addition to her being pregnant, she is afraid of Larraine's betrayal. One day that 'Raine is in her house, she experiences "her nervous turmoil" and "found her eyes fixed on Larraine's throat" (63). The same night she dreams that "Raine's white neck" was as big as a big water standpipe (63). This erotic dream perhaps offers the suggestiveness of her sister's neck which leads to Arvay's aggression.

Hitherto there has been a close investigation of the producers of multiplicity within the texts of *Their Eyes Were Watching God* and *Seraph on the Suwanee*. Multiplicity of meanings is an essential factor to consider a text as a feminine writing. Metaphor and bisexuality are devices by means of which the author is able to achieve multiplicity within her/his texts.

There are certainly other devices that produce proliferated layers of meanings in addition to different signifiers. Hurston's texts hold this capacity. They are overflowed with metaphors and other devices such as pun. Furthermore, they are not vacuous of bisexuality. As it was presumed metaphors of the pear tree, horizon and mud point to Janie's search for fulfillment. In *Seraph*, the notion of Arvay's fragmented self as well as multiple subjectivities is introduced by means of the metaphor of the sea. The metaphor of the mulberry tree plays the role of her source of revelation and realization within this novel. Throughout the next discussion of this chapter, an introduction toward the notion of openness is presented as it is another significant element of a text that should be considered while reading it via the theories of Cixous.

3.2. Emphasis on Openness

Openness is the absence of restraining control in the narrative. There is less severe grammatical observation or syntactic organization within the text. The course of writing is circular and fluidity is recognized throughout it. The structures of both of the selected texts are not completely grammatical. There are numerous shifts between the narration and the conversations. The conversations are inscribed in informal and oral speech form. According to Jones, Hurston weaves elements of oral tradition into her stories (187). Written in the Black Southern vernacular, the conversations do not follow exact grammatical structure even in *Seraph on the Suwanee* that its main characters are white. According to Hazel V. Carby, *Seraph* is imbued with "black figures." He argues that "the language is identical---whole phrases are lifted from the mouth of a black character in an earlier novel and inserted into the mouth of the white Meserve family" (Cited in Hurston, *Seraph* ix). Tate asserts the aforementioned fact by stating: "Hurston must have intended *Seraph's* white characters to sound like Eatonville blacks" (Cited in Bloom 150). In this manner, Hurston has resisted the capitalist and racist patterns restrain her from mingling diction with colloquialism or whiteness and blackness.

Another characteristic of an open narrative is that characters do not repress themselves; they open their minds and mouths and overflow their desires. Janie has been on a search to fulfill her dreams from the beginning and continues her quest until she achieves them. Although Arvay represses her desires at first, she learns to overflow them at last due to realization of her power.

Openness bears the capability to suggest a close relationship with dismantling binary oppositions and undermining the conventional reproductive roles. In the selected novels for the research, a number of binary appositions are dismantled. The established gender roles are undermined especially in *Their Eyes Were Watching God*. Janie does not submit to the sexual constructions imposed on her anymore and rebels against them by marrying Tea Cake who is poor and twelve years younger than her. In addition she gains her voice. She also breaks the oppressions and overthrows the authorities. She goes on further to emancipate herself from Tea Cake's possessive love that she loves the best and the most. Occasionally Arvay attempts to emancipate herself from Jim's dominance. According to Janet Melo-Thaiss these subversions are impossible unless they "take place in an open space of a feminine libidinal economy" ("Viva L'orange: Writing in the open and outlawed space of a Feminine Economy"). Therefore, femininity provides an openness that makes resistance possible.

Both Arvay and Janie long a free bond; in other words they thirst for a mutual and marital relationship that is open. By means of such openness in their relations with their husbands they will not be oppressed. In addition, no stereotypes are opposed on them in the form of gender roles. Janie is not involved in drudgery on the field and Arvay is not restricted in the kitchen. Janie is not located on "a high pedestal" or Arvay in her bedroom. Besides they hope to reveal their thoughts and feelings without the fear of being repressed by their husbands.

Therefore, a particular territory is provided for them which in Melo-Thaiss's terms is "a space of finite (im)possibilities for living and being" ("*Viva L'orange*: Writing in the open and outlawed space of a Feminine Economy").

Throughout this chapter the notions of multiplicity and openness have been argued. The thesis has inspected them since they are momentous in a Cixousian reading of a text. It is argued that multiplicity and openness are the existent elements in the texts of *Their Eyes Were Watching God* and *Seraph on the Suwanee*. Throughout the next chapter the thesis is going to study the element of body and voice as well as the notion of resisting patriarchy.

CHAPTER FOUR

I Was Born with All I Ever Needed to Handle Your Case

A highly substantial characteristic of writing, Cixous thinks, is mingling it with voice. She

claims that she can sense femininity within a text by means of the privilege of voice (Cixous,

Clément 92). Another mode of Cixousian study and any other post-structuralist or

deconstructionist study is rebellion against hierarchies. As reviewed in chapter two, Cixous

attempts to survey the binary oppositions within cultural arenas including writing. She

necessitates the subversion of binary oppositions, which results in dismantling patriarchy.

They are built upon the binary set of Man/Woman, she asserts, and are spread to other aspects

of culture. But this is not the only aspect of a patriarchal culture. Dismantling them is not the

only way to rebel against it, either. Another evident factor of a male-dominated culture is the

gender roles that are opposed on people within such a system. Patriarchal institutions are

present in the world of literature, as well. In a deconstructionist method the subjects in process

are responsible for dismantling this oppression.

 Throughout this chapter, the thesis is going to investigate the notions of voice, body and

resisting patriarchy. It aims to examine if voice is privileged in *Their Eyes Were Watching*

God and *Seraph on the Suwanee*. Furthermore, the notion of resistance will be perused. In

order to achieve the second goal, the thesis has to scrutinize the binary oppositions. Most

significant of all, it explores if patriarchy is challenged. The other notable issue that this thesis

considers is challenging the imposed gender roles and other forms of oppression.

89

4.1. Body as a Site of Resistance

Their Eyes Were *Watching God* and *Seraph on the Suwanee* are highly sensual texts as there are numerous references to corporeality and sensual longings within them. Indeed, they might have been considered as very sensual texts in their times of publication that was 1937 and 1948. Hurston has put into practice what Cixous impels women to do, to resist patriarchy by means of pushing their bodies into writing. Within the following quotation, Cixous appraises women's writing and its subversive quality:

> Women have almost everything to write about femininity: about their sexuality, that is to say, about the infinite and mobile complexity of their becoming erotic, about the lightning ignitions of such a minuscule-vast region of their body, not about destiny but about the adventure of such an urge, . . . Women's body with a thousand and one fiery hearths, when – shattering censorship and yokes – she lets it articulate the proliferation of meanings that runs through it in every direction.
> (Cixous, Clément *The Newly Born Woman* 94)

Through her words, Cixous proclaims that women are aware of their bodies and their longings. This quotation seems to be a defense against psychoanalysts such as Freud who have endeavored to define women's eroticism via their own patriarchal theories. In addition, she hails women to write their bodies in order to resist omission.

Hurston has incorporated the experiences that a woman undergoes relating to her body and gender in her novels. In addition, Zadie Smith approves that Hurston's fame is not the result of the Black Female Literary Tradition, but it is her own self that makes her exceptional. According to Smith, she could express "human vulnerability as well as strength, lyrical without sentiment, romantic and yet rigorous and one of the truly eloquent writers of sex is as exceptional among black women writers as Tolstoy is among white male writers" (8). Within this quotation, Smith asserts that Hurston is not involved with racial issues as her

90

counterparts; instead she is concerned with the notion of reproductive roles and gender problems.

To detect the existence of body in the selected texts, the thesis aims to commence with *Their Eyes Were Watching God.* The readers are encountered with the first exposure of body early in the novel. This paragraph depicts Janie's tantalizing body just as Janie enters Eatonville in her coveralls:

> The men noticed her firm buttocks like she had grape fruits in her hip pockets; the great rope of black hair swinging to her waist and unraveling in the wind like a plume; then her pugnacious breasts trying to bore holes in her shirt. They, the men, were saving with the mind what they lost with the eye. The women took the faded shirt and muddy overalls and laid them away for remembrance. It was a weapon against her strength and if it turned out of no significance, still it was a hope that she might fall to their level some day. (Hurston, *Their Eyes Were Watching God* 2)

There are disputable points that have to be discussed regarding this passage. The first point to be mentioned is that the story does not depict "an artist as an individual of high sensitivity with a portable pedestal" as Kubitschek convincingly argues, "but as a middle-aged, blue-jeaned woman talking with neighbors" (109). Through the portrayal of a woman who enters a communal scene at the outset of the novel, Hurston is therefore deconstructing issues of class and gender via her heroine, Janie. These first three pages are competent to display Janie's power to confront with the oppressive attitudes of society. Her beauty combined with strength is threatening to Eatonville's social system as the representative of American hierarchical structure. Tom McGlamery asserts that Janie's body parts have to be considered as "markers of an essentially undiminished "strength" that both sets in motion the anarchy at the heart of Eatonville and protects her from its effects" (98). Thus, Mc Glamery tries to refute the theory of gaze as a sign of power. He delineates his idea by uttering that:

"Watchers are passive, weak, desirous, envious, feckless, helpless, ignorant, and enthralled."

He considers spectating as a significance of "want" and states that "power belongs to the object of attention, who is often, in fact, God-like" (98). The narrator's persuasive claim that appears immediately after the mentioned paragraph within *Their Eyes* is capable to prove the argument about Janie's body as a sign and site of her empowerment: "But nobody moved, nobody spoke, nobody even thought to swallow spit until after her gate slammed behind her" (Hurston 2).

When Janie hears women's laughter from outside she utters: "Well, Ah see Mouth-Almighty is still sittin' in de same place. And Ah reckon they got *me* up in they mouth now" (Hurston, *Their Eyes* 5). Just like Hurston that uses Janie's hair and her other corporal organs to indicate her beauty, Janie uses mouth; a reproductive part through which one speaks and eats to signify a woman who passes judgments on her.

Nearly the end of the chapter, Janie starts to narrate her story to Phoeby, since she views her as her "intimate" friend. Moreover, Phoeby is considered as her representative therefore Janie can "communicate with the community" through her (Mc Glamery 112). She tells Phoeby: "Ah don't mean to bother with tellin' 'em nothin', Phoeby. 'Tain't worth de trouble. You can tell 'em what Ah say if you wants to. Dat's just de same as me 'cause mah tongue is in mah friend's mouf" (6). The last statement could be regarded as a metaphor since there are hidden meanings beneath its surface. Jan Beneš points to the existence of a "homoerotic" vision in "Mah tongue is in mah friend's mouf" by means of which Hurston attempts to sensualize Janie's narrative (25). In addition, it depicts a kind of union that in McGlamery's words, "provides an image of generative coitus and narrative intimacy and trust" (122). Hence, Janie achieves reproduction through storytelling instead of childbearing.

Right in the next chapter, one of the most sensual scenes in American Literature is revealed in Kaplan's view (*The Erotics*, 115). It portrays Janie's first erotic pleasure combined with her first self-revelation while Phoeby is listening hungrily when "the night time put on flesh and blackness" (Hurston, *Their Eyes* 10). The following paragraphs elucidate how a young girl fantasizes both marriage and intimacy. Moreover, they are capable to reveal that a woman is willing to experience them in a natural way.

> It was a spring afternoon in West Florida. Janie had spent most of the day under a blossoming pear tree in the back-yard. She had been spending every minute that she could steal from her chores under that tree for the last three days. That was to say, ever since the first tiny bloom had opened. It had called her to come and gaze on a mystery. From barren brown stems to glistening leaf-buds; from the leaf-buds to snowy virginity of bloom. It stirred her tremendously. How? Why? It was like a flute song forgotten in another existence and remembered again. What? How? Why? This singing she heard that had nothing to do with her ears. The rose of the world was breathing out smell. It followed her through all her waking moments and caressed her in her sleep. It connected itself with other vaguely felt matters that had struck her outside observation and buried themselves in her flesh. Now they emerged and quested about her consciousness.
>
> She was stretched on her back beneath the pear tree soaking in the alto chant of the visiting bees, the gold of the sun and the panting breath of the breeze when the inaudible voice of it all came to her. She saw a dust-bearing bee sink into the sanctum of a bloom, the thousand sister-calyxes arch to meet the love embrace and the ecstatic shiver of the tree from root to tiniest branch creaming in every blossom and frothing with delight. So this was a marriage! She had been summoned to behold a revelation. Then Janie felt a pain remorseless sweet that left her limp and languid. (Hurston, *Their Eyes* 10-11)

The first paragraph reveals Janie's sensual awakening. The "bloom" is a sign of Janie's burgeoning libido. She questions the birth of natural elements by asking: "What? How? Why?" All of the elements of song, music, nature and literary effects are interwoven together in a dazzling way. The whiteness and purity of the blossoms are compared to a young virgin and nature is compared to a rose which is disseminating its lure odor around. In addition to the previously mentioned similes, there are several other terms that point to marital bliss. The "bees" and "blooms" that astounds Janie, the "panting breath of the breeze," "the love embrace," "ecstatic shiver," that is "creaming" and "frothing with delight," "a pain remorseless sweet," as well as being "limp and languid" contain suggestive overtones, which indicate how Janie, as a typical woman idealizes marriage by means of her imagination and intuitions (Hurston, *Their Eyes* 10-11). Cixous's words endorse this case where she states: "Women's imaginary is inexhaustible, like music, painting, writing: their stream of phantasms is incredible" (*Signs*, Vol.1 No.4 875). Cixous's proclamation justifies both Hurston and Janie's capacity of inexhaustible illusion.

Influenced by the previous scenes, Janie commences her search for love and fulfillment immediately, when she witnesses "flies tumbling and singing, marrying and giving in marriage" in the kitchen (Hurston, *Their Eyes*11). McGlamery argues that this recent scene is more debatable than the bee imagery since it "incorporates elements of communal play, role interchange, and hierarchical dissolution." Thus, it displays a community with no gender limits where a woman is allowed to enter the plays and is not supposed to "class off" (105).

Upon witnessing Janie letting Johnny Taylor kiss her, Nanny pushes Janie into marriage with Logan Killicks because she regards what has happened as harmful and threatening. Nanny's aim is to protect Janie from everything that harmed her Leafy, Janie's mother (Hurston, *Their Eyes* 12). Upon Janie's protest and sob, Nanny starts to narrate the story of her enslavement and Leafy's being assaulted to Janie. Hereby, Nanny proclaims her theory of black woman's enslavement that has been always the site of critics' discussions:

> Honey, de white man is de ruler of everything as fur as Ah been able tuh find out. Maybe it's some place away off in de ocean where de black man is in power, but we don't know nothin' but what we see. So de white man throw down de load and tell de nigger man tuh pick it up. He pick it up because he have to, but he don't tote it. He hand it to his womenfolks. *De nigger woman is de mule uh de world so fur as Ah can see.* Ah been prayin' fuh it tuh be different wid you. Lawd, Lawd, Lawd! (Hurston, *Their Eyes Were Watching God* 14, *emphasis added*)

Through this passage, the distribution of power is classified according to categorization of gender and race. In this gender classification, the black woman has been allotted the lowest level. Thus, she becomes double-exploited as a result of being both black and female. Nanny continues her speech by narrating how she was exploited, assaulted and impregnated by his white master until the abolishment of slavery. She utters how she underwent an assault by her master after childbirth for the last time: ""But pretty soon he let on he forgot somethin' and run into mah cabin and made me let down mah hair for de last time. He sorta wropped his hand in it, pulled mah big toe, lak he always done, and was gone after de rest lak lightning"" (Hurston, *Their Eyes*17). Throughout these lines, Hurston applies euphemism to indicate the harsh assault that Nanny underwent. Another point about these sentences is that Nanny does not feel the confidence within herself to resist enslavement perhaps because of the historical era or as a result of her acceptance of the situation. After her own story, Nanny narrates the story of Leafy being attacked to Janie which is the main reason why Janie's awakening sensuality frightens Nanny.

In addition to glorifying the beauty of her heroine, Hurston praises the attractive qualities of other women in her story on some occasions. There are two paragraphs in chapter six where she delineates other female characters' beauty and femininity. The first scene is displayed as Daisy enters Joe Starks's store porch. The definition of her manners is intriguing:

Daisy is walking in a drum tune. You can almost hear it by looking at the way she walks. She is black and she knows that white clothes look good on her, so she wears them for dress up. She's got those black eyes with plenty shiny white in them that makes them shine like brand new money and she knows what God gave women eyelashes for, too. Her hair is not what you might call straight. It's negro hair, but it has a kind of white flavor. Like the piece of string out of a ham. It's not ham at all, but it's been around ham and got the flavor. It was spread down thick and heavy over her shoulders and looked just right under a big white hat.

(Hurston, Their Eyes 68)

This passage is unique in its attempt to celebrate black features. It is deconstructive in the sense that it does not follow the ordinary western male texts that praise white skin, blue eyes and blonde hair. It also indicates a woman's awareness of her own beauty, which is a meaningful factor in order to value one's own femininity. A further disputable point lies in Hurston's attempt to compare Daisy's eyes to money and her hair to food. These items along with intimacy are the objectives of almost all being's avarice. *Their Eyes* is replete with images that are related to food or mouth, a digestive as well as oral organ. In addition to the presence of "Mouth-Almighty," a gossiping figure who has got Janie in her mouth (Hurston 5), or a community who "passed nations through their mouths" as Mc Glamery also reviews, "back parts" of the community's minds are "chewed up" and "swallowed with relish" (Hurston, *Their Eyes* 2). Janie's hips look like grape fruits. The other similar scenes are Pearl Stone's mouth opening as well as Mrs. Sumpkins suckling her teeth (Hurston, *Their Eyes* 3). Mc Glamery considers these points as results of "lack of emotional and intellectual resources for dealing with the vision of Janie" (97). Yet the existence of similar visions about other women like Daisy is an evidence of such attitudes toward tantalizing characters.

Joe Starks (Jody) confines Janie in several ways. He inflicts wearing kerchief on her head. In addition, he restricts her between the borders of his mansion and store, forbidding her from participating in community gatherings or delivering a speech on such occasions and even enjoying the stories or lying contests that are performed on his store porch. It is one of these lying contests that Mrs. Boggle's arrives with her "blushing air of coquetry" despite of her being "many times a grandmother" (Hurston, *Their Eyes* 69). Joe demands Janie to go and take her orders in spite of her enthusiasm for hearing "the rest of the play-acting" (70). Janie's irritation is followed by a quarrel over a bill, which ends in Joe's humiliating Janie and accusing her of the inconvenience. Janie accedes that she has no other way than to submit and their marriage is in this way troubled. She ascertains that:

> The spirit of marriage left the bedroom and took to living in the parlor. It was there to shake hands whenever company came to visit, but it never went back inside the room again. So she put something in there to represent the spirit like a Virgin Mary image in a church. The bed was no longer a daisy-field for her and Joe to play in. It was a place where she went and laid down when she was sleepy and tired.
>
> (Hurston, *Their Eyes* 71)

These lines convey Janie's lack of marital bliss in her marriage. The "spirit of marriage" could be considered as a metaphoric term regarding marital relations between Janie and her husband in the researcher's point of view. The "Virgin Mary" is the significance of Janie who is deprived of a satisfactory marital intimacy and thus does not reach sensual fulfillment in her marriage.

Occasionally, Hurston's marionettes insult and degrade each other by means of words that are borne with erotic overtones. Jody's arrogance restrains him from admitting his aging that is demonstrated in his weakening knees and ankles, belly that "sagged like a load suspended from his loins" and absent eyes. Therefore, he does his best to decrease his anxieties by revolving the gazing eyes from his own body to Janie's. He denigrates her by calling her "no young pullet" or "ole hen" (Hurston, *Their Eyes* 77). The last time that he ventures to scorn Janie in front of community's eyes, he alleges that Janie is as old as the biblical "Methusalem" due to her failure in cutting the tobacco straightly. Janie refuses to remain silent this time and argues: "When you git through tellin' me how tuh cut uh plug uh tobacco, then you kin tell me whether mah behind is on straight or not" (78). Additionally, she accuses Joe of "talkin' under people's clothes" and thereafter she declares that:

> But Ah'm uh woman every inch of me, and Ah know it. Dat's uh whole lot more'n *you* kin say. You big-bellies round here and put out a lot of brag, but 'taint nothing to it but yo' big voice. Humph! Talkin' 'bout *me* lookin' old! When you pull down yo' britches, you look lak de change uh life. (Hurston, *Their Eyes* 79)

By calling Janie "Methusalem," Jody is falsely accusing Janie of reproductive incapability and this is indeed another attempt to transmit the attentions to Janie. Janie cannot stand his challenges anymore, thus enters the battlefield to defend her femininity as well as sensuality. She assures that she is young, healthy and "woman" (Hurston, *Their Eyes* 79). This case is referent to Irigaray's comment about women's libido. Irigaray claims that women's pleasure is multiple and more than men as the result of their multiple reproductive organs (Irigaray 233).

Tea Cake is Janie's man of dreams and their marriage leads to Janie's fulfillment. This is not because of his "full, lazy eyes with the lashes curling sharply away like drawn scimitars" or his "lean, over-padded shoulders." He seems to Janie "like the love thoughts of women" and reminds her of "a bee to a blossom in the spring." In addition, Janie's intuition is that Tea Cake "was a glance from God" (Hurston, *Their Eyes* 106). Tea Cake's appealing manners are basically the results of his naturalness and unconventionality. Since he does not believe in hierarchical system of values like the other members of their society, he falls in love with Janie who is nearly a decade older than him, admires Janie's beauty and reminds this to her, combs her hair and even scratches the dandruff from her head (103). Therefore, they marry and thereafter "the two began an organic and passionate affair," leaving Eatonville for the muck of the Everglades (King 56).

On some occasions Janie uses her body's roughness to resist the disloyalties and infidelities. Janie tries to beat Tea Cake, when he impertinently returns to Janie after his relationship with Nunkie is uncovered. Janie's physical attack is a remedy to her natural jealousy and she continues the struggle until both of them submit, reunite and sleep "in sweet exhaustion." The narrator reports Janie and Tea Cake's physical confrontation as appears here:

> They wrestled on until they were doped with their own fumes and emanations; till their clothes had been torn away; till he hurled her to the floor and held her there melting her resistance with the heat of his body, doing things with their bodies to express the inexpressible ;....(Hurston, *Their Eyes* 137)

The last site of body in *Their Eyes Were Watching God* to be mentioned regards Mr. and Mrs. Turner. For Janie, love and marital bliss are interconnected; hence the second is a sign of the existence of love. Love paves her way to reach sensual fulfillment and thus self-realization. In contrast to Janie and Tea Cake, Mr. and Mrs. Turner couple do not have a satisfactory and respectable marital life due to their loveless marriage. Consequently, Mr. Turner says Tea Cake: "Ah reckon you ain't 'cause dey all passed on befo' dis one wuz born. ain't had no luck at all wid our chillun. We lucky to raise him. He's de last stroke of exhausted nature" (144). The phrase "exhausted nature" refers to the lack of natural generative satisfaction in Turner couple.

The thesis has perused references of sensuality and corporeal issues within Hurston's *Their Eyes Were Watching God* hitherto. From this point on, the significance of body in *Seraph on the* Suwanee is under the scrutiny. The novel starts with an almost lengthy introduction of Sawley, its history, people and their manners. Then the heroine of the story enters the scene while the spectatorship is focused on her. The people there sit in judgment like the very people in Eatonville. Unlike Janie who is portrayed as a black beauty, Arvay is a white girl but seemingly unconscious about her beauty at the outset. Though her shape is not desirable in her hometown; Sawley, she is extremely pretty according to her creator's appraisal. She seems not to be highly tantalizing but she is "delicate-made" (4). According to Hurston's praise:

> Arvay was lean-made in every way. No heavy-hipped girl below that extremely small waist, and her legs were long and slim-made instead of much-admired "whiskey-keg" look to her legs that was common. She had plenty of long light yellow hair with a low wave and gulf blue eyes. Arvay had a fine-made kind of nose and mouth and face shaped like an egg laid by a leghorn pullet, with a faint spread of pink around her upper cheeks. True, she was said to be so slim that a man would have to shake the sheets to find her in bed, but there were many around Sawley who were willing to put themselves into trouble of making a thorough search of the bed every night. (Hurston, *Seraph* 4)

The timid Arvay falls in love with the young new pastor of the town. But he later marries Arvay's robust-looking sister; Larraine. After that time, according to Claudia Tate, Arvay suffers from secret "mental adultery" (Cited in Bloom 144). She later tries to compensate her guilt by "turning away from the world" and "self-denying," which results in her sensual repression and hysterical attacks and are exposed in the form of spasms (Hurston, *Seraph* 3). She has contracted spasms at the beginning of her youth and it is revealed that Maria, Arvay's mother had also spasms when she was a young girl. Her seizures can be considered as a form of physical resistance toward her urging womanhood and an attack toward the eyes of the community who criticize her calmness, refusal of marriage and renunciation. They are addressed as "fit(s)" in the informal language of people (6). Checked in *the Longman Advanced American Dictionary*, "fit" bear two related meanings. The first one which is connected to emotion describes: "a very strong emotion that you cannot control" and the second is: "Stop Being Conscious" followed by a broader definition of "a short period of time when someone stops being conscious and cannot control their body because their brain cannot work correctly" (607). It is notable that the narrator of the story defines for the reader: "It was usually taken as a sign of a girl being "highstrung". Marriage would straighten her out" (Hurston, *Seraph* 6). From the information above, it can be presumed that Arvay developed spasms or fits because she could not control her strong emotions, almost libidinal that hurt her. Arvay's mental situation is to some extent similar to Dora, a young girl who suffered from hysteria and was psychoanalyzed by Sigmund Freud. Later, Cixous studies the case of Dora and tries to undermine what Freud tried to judge on women's desire. In some way or other, Cixous has glorified Dora and has written a play based on her to acknowledge her resistance toward patriarchal institutions. In *The Newly Born Woman* she writes:

> The hysterics are my sisters. As Dora, I have been all the characters she played, the ones who killed her, the one who shivers when she ran through them, and in the end I got away, having been Freud one day, Mrs. Freud another, also Mr. K . . . , Mrs. K . . .- and the wound Dora inflicted on them. [...] But I am what Dora would have been if woman's history had begun. (Cixous & Clément 99)

Arvay's procrastination in submitting a definite answer frustrates her suitor, Jim. Indeed, she tries to oppose the conventional expectations that urge her to marry and have children. Therefore, Jim seeks help from Joe Kelsey, his pet Negro and he advised Jim to handle her like a horse, "get the bridle in her mouth" and ride her hard (Hurston, *Seraph* 46)! This is a similar version of the "mule" metaphor and exposes a brutal attitude toward women who are not willing to submit to male-dominated conditions. Therefore, Jim rapes Arvay two weeks prior their wedding day to win her acquiescence. According to Tate, unfortunately, Arvay is unable to understand that the attack as a "scenario" to make her bound to Jim (Cited in Bloom 144).

Jim is successful in binding Arvay to himself. After the intimacy, Arvay tries to get close to Jim deliberately. Tate writes that: "The failure to recognize their mutual insecurities binds them in a sadomasochistic cycle of sexual aggression and submission, which the attack foreshadows. According to Tate, this defensive pattern of erotic attachment defines their marriage for more than twenty years" (Cited in Bloom 145). Arvay's mental condition after the premature affair is narrated in this way:

> Jim's urging was altogether unnecessary. Some unknown power took hold of Arvay. She pressed her body tightly against his, fitting herself into him as closely as possible. A terrible fear came over her that he might somehow vanish away from her arms, and she sought to hold him by the tightness of her embrace and her flood of kisses. It seemed a great act of mercy when she found herself stretched on the ground again with Jim's body weighing down upon her. Somehow, she seemed not to be able to get close enough to him. Never, never, close enough. She must eat him up, and absorb him within herself. Then he could never leave again.
>
> (Hurston, *Seraph* 56)

Jim is very cruel in irritating Arvay and addressing their affair as a "rape" just as Arvay thinks. Arvay does not act consciously and just goes away with Jim. She is not even sure that they would get married. Jim's reference to intimacy as a "rape" connotes his sexual oppressiveness similar to other men who become successful in domination over women by means of opposing it. Jim speaks to Arvay about the event in this way: "And it would not have done you a damn bit of good. Just a trashy waste of good time and breath. Sure you was raped, and that ain't all. You're going to keep on getting raped. You couldn't be hollering for your Pa every day for the rest of your life, could you?" (Hurston, *Seraph* 56-7). Therefore, Jim foreshadows Arvay's enslavement in their life through his words. According to Susan Meisenhelder, Arvay is "ultimately reduced to a lustful object in her relationship with Jim..." (Cited in Jones 161).

There are hints of homoerotic drives within the novel. They are revealed in the form of Arvay's aggression and hate toward her disgusting sister Larraine. This sense haunts Arvay during her first pregnancy. It is also followed by a homoerotic aggressive and scary dream at the same night.

> In her nervous turmoil, brought on by disappointment and memories of other frustrations, somehow Arvay found her eyes fixed on Larraine's throat. That night Arvay had a strange dream. She saw 'Raine's white neck. It was huge like the standpipe at the water works, and down its long length blood was running from a huge gash near the top.
>
> Another night Arvay dreamed that she was in a beautiful forest of trees and very happy. Music and singing were coming to her from unseen voices. Suddenly the instruments and voices hushed as if in terrible fear. In the silence, Larraine came walking through the woods. A tiger leaped upon Larraine and tore her throat away. Great streams of blood ran down and clotted between Larraine's breasts.
>
> (Hurston, *Seraph on the Suwanee* 63-64)

Arvay possesses a latent power of which she is unaware until she reaches to a self-revelation and fulfillment at the end of the novel on the sea. Her husband recognizes her astonishing power but never lets Arvay notice his wonder. Arvay's sensual, biological and feminine power is hidden and displayed in her eyes at the same time. She is capable of conjuring Jim with her eyes. According to the narrator:

> Arvay's eyes had some strange power to change like that when she was stirred for him. Each time that she succumbed to his love making, Arvay's eyes gradually changed from that placid blue to a misty greenish-blue like the waters of the sea at times and at places. It warmed him, it burned him and bound him. But Jim did not consider himself weak in being overcome like that. He placed Arvay as having powers that few women on earth had. The strange thing was that she did know her own strength. (Hurston, *Seraph* 106)

There is an occasion when Arvay tries to expel Jim firmly, which is after Earl's death. Perhaps, she recognizes Jim as responsible for Earl's being murdered. Arvay refuses to accept what has happened to her son and resists entering normal life. Jim attempts to confront with her repudiation by imposing a challenge on her. In this way, Arvay begins "sinking, sinking, down through the mattress, through the floor and through the world on some soft cloudy material, and drifting off through the rim-bones of space" and becomes "departed from herself and knew nothing until she came to earth again and found herself in the familiar bed" (Hurston, *Seraph* 158). This paragraph reveals another sign of consideration with physicality within the selected novel.

Arvay disagrees with Angeline's getting company, since she does not wish for her daughter to be entangled in the same trap of sexual exploitation like herself. Angeline and her fiancé's outspoken manner in talking to each other worries Arvay to an extraordinary extent because of her experience of being attacked two weeks before the marriage, which ends in her sexual victimization. This issue reminds the readers of Nanny's stressful concern for Janie as she is afraid of her young innocent granddaughter to be abused by an oppressor. In addition, this excerpt is a sign of Hurston's involvement with women's corporeality in her works.

As mentioned formerly, Arvay realizes her power, mainly her corporeal power finally. She recognizes what are hidden in her body and flesh. She learns that Angie's beauty is not inherited from Jim but she has received her female beauty from Arvay. In addition, she discovers that Kenny has also inherited his musical talent from his mother. She contemplates upon the wonders of human body and her own body as particular:

> The good that was in her flesh had taken form. Angeline, female beauty, had come out of her, and Kenny, as handsome a boy as you would find anywhere. Kenny had come bringing the music part inside her that she had never had a chance to show herself. ... He [Kenny] represented those beautiful sounds that she used to hear from nowhere as she played around with her doll under the mulberry tree.... Human flesh was full of mysteries and a wonderful and unknown thing.
>
> (Hurston, *Seraph* 350)

According to Jan Beneš, Arvay seeks new roles for her body in the end as she notices the multiple powers residing in her. She willingly returns to her turbulent marriage with Jim in order to become an equal partner, finally. Arvay's firm determination differentiates her from the early hesitant woman of the beginning of the novel (7). As a consequence, Arvay undergoes different processes regarding her body to approach self-actualization. She can expose her power in protecting Jim like a watchful mother (Hurston, *Seraph* 351).

Similar to Janie that is led to wearing overalls because of living and working on the muck, Arvay is forced to wearing "a pair of blue jeans that fishermen wore, two blue shirts, and the tall rubber sea-boots" (Hurston, *Seraph* 323). She has to confront with Jim in fishing clothes and realizes it while she is preparing to talk to him determinedly. These are Arvay's first attempts to shake the basis of patriarchal authority which is incarnated within Jim. She does not decorate herself with "female things" and the blue working shirt stands "between her hips and her knees" (Hurston, *Seraph* 345). Nevertheless, she becomes Jim's object of spectatorship. She gains her self-confidence in every possible way and commences the talk with Jim, since she possesses "some weapon" and the necessary equipment to "handle" Jim, which is her body (Hurston, *Seraph* 347).

Hurston's obsession with the notion of sensuality puts her into an unusual trouble. She suffered from the destructive reputation produced by the propaganda against both her personality and literary production, notwithstanding she was vindicated after six months. After the publication of *Seraph on the Suwanee* she was falsely accused of molesting a ten year old child (King 10). According to Tate, in order to prove Hurston's aggressive sexuality, the *Baltimore Afro-American Review* used an excerpt from *Seraph on the Suwanee*, which is uttered by Jim: "I'm just as hungry as a dog for a knowing and a doing love" (Cited in Bloom 153). Tate concentrates on this event as an irony because Hurston aimed to play this novel as a joke on her reader's perspectives on sensuality and womanhood but unfortunately was ended up as a cruel joke played on her own self (Cited in Bloom 153).

Thus far, the thesis has surveyed Hurston's involvement with the notion of body in *Their Eyes Were Watching God* and *Seraph on the Suwanee*. It has been tried to represent possible references throughout both novels to prove Hurston's concern with bodily matters. It was perceived that Janie, the heroine of *Their Eyes Were Watching God* is searching for her full sensual expression (King 59). As a matter of fact, Kaplan has addressed her as a woman who seeks for jouissance (Kaplan, *The Erotics* 137-63). It was perceived that there are definitions of women's body and femininity, as well as the portrayal of their drives in the selected texts. One can see a deliberate portrait of the female features and corporeal descriptions. Through the next discussion the thesis is going to discuss the issue of voice that is a key feature of écriture féminine.

4.2. The Privilege of Voice

In her influential essay "Sorties," Cixous declares that the first element through which the femininity of a text could be understood is the "privilege of *voice*" within (Cixous & Clément 92). To elucidate it more: "*Writing and voice* are entwined and interwoven" so that they are in a process of substitution and interchange. Feminine writing does not stop echoing the act of obtaining the power of speech (Cixous & Clément 92). This is absolutely the case with those of Hurston's works that are selected for this research. First of all there is a privilege of voice. The heroines soon or late acquire the power of speech. Secondly, there are always shifts between the narrations and the dialogues; hence it can be assumed that voice and writing are entwined within these texts.

There are natural elements in *Their Eyes Were Watching God* that foreshadow the importance of voice in Janie's fulfillment. When she spends her spring days under that pear tree, it seems like it was "a flute song forgotten in another existence and remembered again"

(10). She hears and enjoys the sounds of natural elements. It is written that Janie "was soaking in the alto chant of the visiting bees" touched by the "panting breath of the breeze when the inaudible voice of it all came to her" (11). The reader can almost hear the voice of nature represented in these lines; natural vocal elements such as: "flute song," "alto chant," "bees" and "panting breath of breeze" (Hurston, *Their Eyes* 11). These vocal elements also point to the erotic powerful qualities existing in voice. Janie possesses the ability to communicate with nature:

> She knew things that nobody had ever told her. For instance, the words of the trees and the wind. She often spoke to falling seeds and said, "Ah hope you fall on soft ground," because she had heard seeds saying that to each other as they passed. She knew the world was a stallion rolling in the blue pasture of ether. She knew that God tore down the old world every evening and built a new one by sun-up. (Hurston, *Their Eyes* 25)

In addition to the mentioned fact, there are a couple of songs within the text. They are considered as the means to increase the vocal and rhythmic quality of it. According to Cixous, there is always a reverberation of some touchable affecting power in feminine speech as well as in feminine writing. She refers to song as "music of love," which exists in every woman and here it exists in this feminine text written down by a woman. As there is an emphasis on music in Hurston's texts, she has contrived the existence of some songs in both of the novels. One song appears in chapter five of *Their Eyes Were Watching God*, is sung by a woman named Mrs. Boggle. She sings this song in the town's lighting ceremony:

We'll walk in de light, de beautiful light

Come where the dew drops of mercy shine bright

Shine all around us by day and by night

Jesus, the light of the world. (Hurston, *Their Eyes* 46)

The notable point about this song is that a woman sings it. The other song appears in chapter eighteen, when Tea Cake, Janie and their Bahaman friends are around the fire at midnight having a good time. Muck-boy who is asleep suddenly wakes up and begins to chant with the rhythm and everybody repeat the last word of the line":

Yo' mama don't wear no *Draws*

Ah seen her when she took 'em *Off*

She soaked 'em tuh de Santy *Claus*

He told her 'twas aginst de *Law*

To wear dem dirty *Draws* (Hurston, *Their Eyes* 157).

This song, in addition to enhancing the reverberation of Hurston's text, projects a foreshadowing effect. The existence of the term "soaked" is a sign of the flood that Janie and Tea Cake will be trapped within later in the novel. Checked in the Oxford Dictionaries Online, the term *"Draws"* can suggest "an act of pulling again from its holster in order to shoot." Hence, this song attempts to foreshadow shooting and perhaps murder. The other connotation is resulted by means of concentrating on the words *"wears"* and *"Draws"* as well as the phrases "took 'em *Off*" and "against de *Law*." They imply the relation of this song to clothes, perhaps Janie's. If this song is considered in this way, Janie's muddy and unconventional coveralls in which Janie returns to Eatonville are foreshadowed.

The presence of song in *Seraph on the Suwanee* should not be neglected, either. At the first night of their marriage, Arvay and Jim are in their shack among the woods that hear a gentle melody and sounds of guitar played out by Negroes from outside the window (Hurston 58). There is all harmony accompanied with bass and "clear melody" (58). There are instrumentals, blues and spirituals with "a drummy rhythm" performed both by men and women (59). The music produces views, "odors and tastes," "streams of color" and "exotic fruits" (59). These particularities of the music that Arvay hears can convey that voice

108

possesses erotic capabilities similar to vision, and even more than that, it has a sensual

quality. Then there is an old ballad, which is led by a female sound:

> Love, oh, love, Oh careless love
> Goes right to the head like wine
> Broken the heart of many a poor girl
> But you'll never break this heart of mine.
>
> Love, Oh, love, Oh careless love
> Love, Oh, love, Oh careless love
> You cause me to weep, you cause me to moan
> You cause me to leave my happy home. (Hurston, *Seraph* 59)

It is necessary to take into notice that this song is performed through a female voice, as well.

A disputable point about *Their Eyes Were Watching God* is Nanny narrating her own

story. She becomes the narrator of her story. After Detecting Johnny Taylor "lacerating her

Janie with a kiss", "Nanny closed her eyes and nodded a slow, weary affirmation many times

before she gave it a voice" (12). She starts to reveal her worries and wishes to Janie; the

miseries that she has undergone during the enslavement including her sufferings of physical

and racial exploitation, attack and child bearing. According to Cixous statement in *The Newly*

Born Woman, even a woman's political and "theoretical" discourse is not linear; "She involves

her story in history" (92). Hurston gives her characters of *Their Eyes Were Watching God* the

opportunity to emerge their stories. Dolan Hubbard uses the term "(Her)story," perhaps

instead of "history," in his article, to point to the stories that are narrated by Nanny Janie in

Their Eyes Were Watching God (Cited in Bloom, 35-45). Nanny tells "(Her)story" to Janie the

same as what Janie does to her friend Phoeby. Not only Nanny involves "(Her)story" in

history through Janie, but also she tells her daughter's story, Leafy's sufferings and miseries

(Hurston, *Their Eyes*16-20). She aims to reveal these difficulties and provide the securities for

both Leafy and Janie to survive in a racist as well as patriarchal society. She says Janie: "Ah wanted to preach a great sermon about colored women sittin' on high, but they wasn't no pulpit for me" (16). Eventually she preaches her seminal sermon to Janie about the nigger woman being the mule of the world (14). Hence, she delivers a political speech as well as a personal one.

Although Janie is somehow forced to accept the marriage to Logan, she does not remain extremely silent. Three months after her marriage she visits Nanny to express her dissatisfaction with her husband (Hurston, *Their Eyes* 23). Later she speaks her mind to Logan as well and "put words in his held-in fears" by saying: "S'posin' Ah wuz to run off and leave you sometime." The later speech is followed by "Ah might take and find somebody dat did trust me and leave you" (Hurston, *Their Eyes* 30). Logan does not take Janie's warning seriously and keeps on accusing her of her grandmother, mother and anything that she does not choose herself (32). Upon coercing Janie to obey his demands immediately, Janie answers him: "You ain't done me no favor by marryin' me. And if dat's what you call yo'self doin', Ah don't thank you for it" (31). Then she leaves him rebelliously. By marrying Joe Starks, despite his incubus behavior, Janie remains silent most of the time until the day of the rebellion in the store. In spite of her attempts, Janie is forbidden from giving a speech in the public. On the day of the election of the Mayor of Eatonville, when Janie is invited to deliver a speech, suddenly Jody comments: "Thank yuh fuh yo' compliments, but mah wife don't know nothin' 'bout no speech-makin'. Ah never married her for nothin' lak dat. She's uh woman and her place is in de home" (43). Janie pretends to laugh though it was not easy. The narrator states that: "She had never thought of making a speech, and didn't know if she cared to make one at all" (Hurston, *Their Eyes* 43). But then the readers notice that she comes back "feeling cold" that night while Jody was "unconscious of her thoughts" (43). Janie is not satisfied with this deprivation and strives to speak like any other community members in spite of being unconscious about it.

An activity that Janie favors it a lot but is prohibited from participating it is storytelling. Storytelling is regarded as a male-dominated territory in Eatonville, being performed on Joe Starks's store porch. Just as writing has been a male space saved for men as Cixous mentions in her essay "The Laugh of the Medusa," that "sexual opposition" has always served male's profit, storytelling is a domain preserved for the sake of men (*Signs* vol.1 NO.4 883). In this condition, men of Eatonville gather and deliver their stories. Even listening to them is full of excitement for Janie as people reveal "the picture of their thoughts," which is indeed "crayon enlargements of life" (Hurston, *Their Eyes* 51). This implies that storytelling is a way of exposing mind and defining life. Janie is deprived of the right to declare what is going on in her mind, notwithstanding she thinks of good stories and performs them in her mind. She is even restricted from listening to other people's performances by Joe Starks. However, after his death she surpasses the oppressive borders of the phallocentric territory of the porch and pushes herself into the open spaces of the store porch, the fields on the muck and her houses back porch.

A humorous adventure that occupies the story sessions to is Matt Bonner's mule. Everybody has a part in the mule talk. Janie likes it very much and tries to make good stories in her mind as Jody prevented her from indulging in the sessions (Hurston, *Their Eyes* 53). The mule is weak to death and the town's people keep on bothering the poor beast to death. One day that Janie is watching them having fun by bothering the mule, mutters to herself: "They oughta be shamed uh theyselves! Teasin' dat poor brute beast lak they is" (Hurston, *Their Eyes* 56)! Joe hears her and buys the mule with a lower price and then emancipates it. Everybody respects Joe's deed. It is here that Janie attempts to deliver a parodic speech toward Joe. Although her speech seems to be an obsequious praise of Joe, it is a joke that is played on him.

Jody, dat wuz uh mighty fine thing fuh you tuh do. 'Tain't everybody would have thought of it, 'cause it ain't no every thought. Freei'n dat mule makes uh mighty big man outa you. Something like George Washington and Lincoln. Abraham Lincoln, he had de whole United States tuh rule so he freed de Negroes. You got uh town so you freed a mule. You have tuh have power tuh free things and that makes you lak uh king uh something. (Hurston, *Their Eyes* 58)

Upon hearing her speech, a man named Hambo comments on Janie's speech and calls her: "a born orator" continued by she puts "de right words tuh our thoughts" (58). Jody neither pays attention to him nor says a word. The mule has in fact a metaphoric reference to black woman. Indeed, Janie pities herself as she is entrapped in Jody's hands. It does not last long that the mule dies. The carcass is going to be buried in the woods and there is going to be a funeral as if it is a real citizen. Janie likes to go with Jody very much but when she utters her enthusiasm, he rejects by telling her that he goes there himself not just because of that he is a Mayor, but because he is a man. Moreover, he mentions that they need him to deliver speech in the mule's funeral, but Janie is not going to participate as she is a woman, in addition to being the Mayor's wife. Jody goes and delivers a long humorous speech as if he is a pastor preaching a sermon about the mule going to heaven. He comes back to the store full of pleasure while Janie has been sad in the store (Hurston, *Their Eyes* 60-2).

Once Janie dares to break her silence in an attempt to "thrust herself into a conversation" which "she never did before" (Hurston, *Their Eyes* 75). It takes place after Mrs. Tony comes to store begging Joe Starks for food while Starks keeps on telling her that Tony buys groceries every Saturday. Mrs. Robbins answers: "If he buy all dat you talkin' 'bout, Mist' Starks, God knows whut he do wid it. He sho don't bring it home, and me and mah po' chillun is *so* hungry Mist' Starks, please gimme uh lil piece uh meat fuh me and mah chillun" (73). Mrs. Robbins acts like a hungry cat that approaches a pan of meat until Joe cuts a very little piece of meat with stinginess and gives it to her, while she is nagging about people like Joe who do not have pity for a poor woman with children. The men in the store start to criticize women like her harshly, commenting why Tony does not hit her wife that Janie enters the discussion to which Jody reacts by calling Janie "too moufy":

Sometimes God gits familiar wid us womenfolks too and talks His inside business. He told me how surprised He was 'bout y'all turning out so smart after Him makin' yuh different; and how surprised y'll is goin' tuh be if you ever find out you don't know half as much 'bout us as you think you do. It's so easy to make yo' self out God Almighty when you ain't got nothin' tuh strain against but women and chickens. (Hurston, *Their Eyes* 75)

Janie cannot silence herself anymore. She is frustrated with Jody's dominance. Moreover, as Jody is getting older he starts to scorn Janie of becoming old. The day he convicts Janie in the store of cutting the tobacco wrongly and getting as old as "Methusalem," Janie becomes infuriated and emasculates Joe verbally and metaphorically. Her verbal rebellious outburst ends with robbing Jody terribly "of his illusion of irresistible maleness that all men cherish" in the presence of people in the store (Hurston, *Their Eyes* 79):

Naw , Ah ain't no young gal no mo' but den Ah ain't no old woman neither. Ah reckon Ah looks mah age too. But Ah'm uh woman every inch of me, and Ah know it. Dat's uh whole lot more'n you kin say. You big-bellies round here and put out a lot of brag, but 'taint nothing to it but yo' big voice. Humph! Talkin' 'bout me lookin' old! When you pull down yo' britches, you look lak de change uh life.

(Hurston, *Their Eyes* 79)

Depending on these scenes, it can be assumed that Janie gains her tongue back in the store. Joe Starks's store and its porch are male territories where only men can have conversation. It is like the act of "writing" that is a phallogocentric territory for men's exhibition of power. Janie undermines the restraints encumbering her and trespasses the territory reserved for men and embarks on speaking. Since then, fragile from being scorned by

Janie, Jody has kept on living in another room downstairs to be away from Janie. He becomes sick on bed but still does not want to see Janie while different people, some of whom, Jody never spends his time with, come to his house. He is becoming weak and is not under the observation of any doctor. There is just a traditional black sorcery practitioner who tries to heal Jody by for example finding something buried that is against him (Hurston, Their Eyes 84). One morning, Janie determines to go and talk to Jody. It is so difficult for her and she feels "an oxen's foot" standing "on her tongue" (84). It is like what Cixous points to in 'Sorties' about the torture of beginning to speak, which is accompanied with heart beating and "loss of language" (Cixous, Clément 92). Jody resists seeing Janie or talking to her. He demands her to go away as he wants to rest. Janie resists determinedly by saying that: "Naw, Jody, Ah come in heah tuh talk widja and Ah'm goin tuh do it. It's for both of our sakes Ah'm talkin'" (Hurston, *Their Eyes* 85). She starts by admitting her own delinquencies but Jody keeps her point and goes further. When Janie gains back the thread of language she declares that she does not feel sympathy for him as a consequence of his patriarchal deeds. Janie ventures to tell him who she genuinely is before it is "too late" (Hurston, *Their Eyes* 85). Although he lives with Janie for about twenty years, he is so arrogant that does not recognize her wife's honesty. Jody is shocked at the sight of death and yells at Janie to go out as he does not believe her. This situation is just what Cixous calls: "A double anguish, for even if she transgresses, her word almost always falls on the deaf, masculine ear, which can only hear language that speaks in the masculine" (Cixous, Clément 92). Janie's words falls on Jody's "deaf, masculine ear" which does not hear Janie's voice. However, Janie does not move and continues confidently:

> Ah knowed you wasn't gointuh lissen tuh me. You changes everything but nothin' don't change you-not even death. But Ah ain't goin' outa here and Ah ain't gointuh hush. Naw, you goin' tuh listen tuh me one time befo' you die. Have yo' way all yo' life, trample and

mash down and then die ruther than tuh let yo'self heah 'bout it. Listen, Jody, you ain't de Jody ah run off de road wid. You'se whut's left after he died. Ah run off tuh keep house wid you in uh wonderful way. But you wasn't satisfied wid me de way Ah was. Naw! Mah own mind had tuh be squeezed and crowded out tuh make room for yours in me. (Hurston, *Their Eyes* 86)

It was mentioned in the preceding discussions that Nanny is given the opportunity to tell her story and emerge "(Her)story" into history. Like Nanny, Janie attempts to push "her story into history" by narrating it to Phoeby on the back porch of her house in Eatonville right after her return (Cixous, Clément 92). Storytelling has been another territory, which is reserved for men. She displays her disobedience again by entering another patriarchal field. She does not present her story to a man, but to a woman whose ears are not deaf, hence she can understand a feminine language. When Janie's story was over, Phoeby gives out a heavy breath and commented: "Ah done growed ten feet higher fom jus' listenin' tuh you, Janie. Ah ain't satisfied wid mahself no mo'…. Nobody better not criticize yuh in mah hearin" (Hurston, *Their Eyes* 192).

Another characteristic of the privilege of voice is the existence of dialogues. This is a specification of not only *Their Eyes Were Watching God* but also of *Seraph on the Suwanee*. *Seraph on the Suwanee* is full of dialogues, conversations and shifts between the narrative and conversations just like *Their Eyes Were Watching God*. The text is occasionally rhythmic and the heroine gains her opportunity to speak. As a result of this, there is a connection between voice and writing in the text of *Seraph*.

The interest in music is traced in Arvay as well. Arvay could learn playing the organ. She has a unique ability in playing music and working on melodies and songs, she was invited to take part in Sunday school orchestra and the church's chorus. According to Cixous, song is "the first music of the voice of love, which every woman keeps alive" (Cixous, Clément 93).

She adds by mentioning that "the first nameless love is singing" inside every woman (93). Arvay and Jim's married life is also referred as music according to the narrator: "They played[sic] music on the instrument of life. It was[sic] merely that two or three of the keys were out of fix, and there was[sic] a break in the tune were[sic] they were touched[sic]" (Hurston, *Seraph* 76). It implies that they do not play their instrumental selves in harmony with each other.

Another point in Cixous's essay that can be compared with Arvay's case is the way of a woman's speaking. She declares that when a woman speaks in a meeting, she does not actually "speak", but "she throws her trembling body into the air, she lets herself go, she flies, she goes completely into her voice, she vitally defends the logic of her discourse with her body; her flesh speaks true" (Cixous ,Clément 92). Arvay's emotional problems have been developed into hysteric seizures and fits. She expressed her hidden desires and concealed sufferings not verbally but by means of her body. On a Sunday noon, Jim comes to the Henson's house for lunch as Arvay's resolute suitor. When he starts to talk about Larraine, Arvay has suddenly a bad attack of spasms. Sugar and turpentine have been the means to cure her. Mistakenly, Jim drops the last drops of turpentine into Arvay's right eye instead of the sugar spoon. Arvay reveals her energetic self upon this action:

> Then a hurricane struck the over-crowded parlor. Arvay gave a yell from the very bottom of her lungs and catapulted her body from that sofa. She was all over the room at one time, seemingly, knocking over and upsetting things. Jim heard Brock's footsteps hurrying up the hall just as Arvay got her directions and split out of the door. She collided with her father, rushed on past the temporary obstruction, and vanished down the hall in a cloud of flying yellow hair and pink skirts. Nothing but scream and screech in her wake as she made it to the back porch.
>
> (Hurston, *Seraph* 32)

Afterwards Arvay washes her eye with fresh water and calls Jim a "varmint" and a "scoundrel-beast." Convicting him of pouring the turpentine in her eye on purpose, she expresses her tendency to kill him with a gun. Brock Henson who is impressed by the scene comments: "I never knowed that Arvay had that much life in her" (Hurston, *Seraph* 33). Arvay has many verbal fights with Jim but most of the time she could not reveal her inner world to Jim brilliantly. She speaks to Jim many times to confirm her power over her. For instance, when she talks about Joe Kelsey's moonshine business, or her daughter's performance in the railroad with Kenny, which is conducted by Kenny, Earl's problem and his been putting down into a mental hospital; are all conversations through which Arvay tries to convince Jim.

Now and then, Arvay wonders about Jim's power over him. The night that they are in Tallahassee for Kenny's performance, she insists on leaving there sooner than Jim's expectation. They leave there for Arvay's convenience but Jim revenges Arvay as best as he can because she does not give him the chance to be there up to the last minute. After arriving home, he demands Arvay to serve him. This makes her happy at first because she thought Jim has forgotten everything and she is forgiven. However, a sudden drive makes her to stop and resist Jim's sensual and biological power. Arvay becomes exhausted of Jim's power over herself and needs liberation; hence she begins crying and demands him to go away, saying:

> I can't stand this bondage you got me in. I can't endure no more! I can't never feel satisfied that I got you tied to me, and I can't leave you, and I can't kill you nor hurt you in no way at all. I'm tied and bound down in a burning Hell and no way out that I see. I can't see never no peace of mind. It's a sure enough hard game when you got to die to beat it, but that's just what I aim to do- kill myself!
>
> (Hurston, *Seraph* 218)

Being in Sawley for her mother's funeral ceremony, Carl attempts to pay a visit to her in order to rob her of her money, claiming that she owes a thousand dollars because he has been hurt in her inherited house the night before. Carl's claim is against the law as even if he tells the truth he has trespassed Arvay's lawful territory, notwithstanding he is not telling the truth. By means of the hotel manager's guidance, Arvay is made sure that Carl is trying to extract money from her by means of his deceits; hence she does not submit the one thousand dollars that Carl demands. Outrageous at Arvay's persistence, he threatens her to deliver the matter to a good lawyer, but Arvay does not surrender and ridiculously advises him to use some "mutton tallow," "melt" and "mix" it with some turpentine and grease his back to cure his hurt behind. Arvay is indeed joking though she assures the angry and hopeless Carl that she was not.

Arvay's last influential and convincing conversation to be mentioned here, is her steadfast speaking to her husband Jim on his boat while they are on the sea nearly the end of the novel. Arvay has determined to gain him back; hence she dares to open her heart and reveals her mind. Arvay prepares herself, puts the door of the cabin half-opened and calls him while he is passing there. She tells him that she has something to tell him and Jim acts defensively. She tells Jim: "You can't go down below to sleep tonight, Jim, that is, not until I have a talk with you nohow. You can't go . . ." (Hurston, *Seraph* 346). She repeats herself in another way, and suspends for some time until Jim demands her to talk. Her situation was like Janie's when she wants to talk to Jody while he is on his death bed. Arvay has lost language; she has lost the words. She gasps, as Cixous tells, out of "Suspenses and silences," makes her voice loose and "rend[s] it with cries" (Cixous , Clément 92).

> Arvay realized that she had the floor, and it threw her into a vast panic. That chance that
> she had yearned for through long terrible months was in her hand. But her speech of
> explanations and review had flown out of her presence and was blowing off somewhere

over the big ocean. She didn't have any ideas. She didn't even have any words. She was on the point of crying. (Hurston, *Seraph*346)

Upon repeating that Jim should not go down and they have to have a conversation, Jim says: ""Arvay, do you realize that you are giving orders to the captain of a ship? And on the high seas at that? That's mutiny which is a high crime punishable by death, and instant death if I feel like it. And then on top of that, it's pretty damned biggity and imposing"" (Hurston, *Seraph* 346). But Arvay does not hesitate anymore and goes on speaking and demanding Jim to stop and listen. Jim, who is surprised at Arvay's courage, convicts her of finding a "weapon." Arvay's reaction to his claims and their conversation goes on like this:

> ARVAY: "Do I need any more weapon than I already got? Did I ever need any different?" Arvay shot an impudent and challenging look at Jim.
> ARVAY: "Maybe the reason you never see no bear-cat with hip-pockets is because he don't have no need to tote no pistol with him. I was born with all I ever needed to handle your case."
> [. . .]
> JIM. "There now! The mule done kicked Rucker!" Jim exploded, and Arvay caught him eye-balling her in a new way.
> JIM. "You're mighty plague-goned impudent and sassy these days." He gave Arvay a strong under-eye look.
> JIM. "Who's been pomping you up so? Who's been telling you that you're pretty?"
> ARVAY. "Jim Meserve, that's who."
> JIM. "Oh, is *that* the case? When did I tell you all that, Arvay?"
> ARVAY. "Ever since I knowed you ... in one way or another. Aw, I ain't near so dumb as I used to be. I can read your writing. Actions speak louder than words."
>
> (Hurston, *Seraph* 346-7)

Arvay has gained power by means of her voice and thus she speaks. A weapon that Jim thinks Arvay has found and she admits to possess is nothing but her voice. According to the narrative, she is scared and she trembles when she decides firmly to throw "her trembling body" (Cixous, Clément 92). "But one time in her life, she wanted to fully express herself in words and let Jim know how she had improved and changed" (Hurston, *Seraph* 348). She succeeds in having a good talk with Jim, confesses her dumbness and displays her empowered self at last.

4.3. Resisting Patriarchy

One of the most critical aspects of Cixous's studies is "Patriarchal Binary Thought" (Eagleton, *Working* 146). As Hélène Cixous inscribes: "Thought has always worked through opposition" (Cixous, Cited in Eagleton 146). The main goal of Cixousian methodology is first to realize how these binary oppositions work and second dismantle the process of these oppositions throughout the text. The patriarchal binary oppositions are closely related to hierarchies, authorities and oppressors. The positive side of a binary opposition, which appears on the left, is the hierarchical side. Deconstruction and subversion are the means to undermine the dichotomies and hierarchies within the text.

Hurston's texts bear the quality of being subversive. Amy Fass Emery argues that Hurston's celebrated folklore "has the power to be aggressively subversive", that it "gives a voice to those on the margins who seek to challenge their oppressors" (328). In addition, Mellisa Harris Perry approves of Zora Neale Hurston's texts, particularly *Their Eyes*, as she asserts that they bear "the task of understanding the heart of a woman and thereby exposes meaningful political truths about hierarchy, oppression, and liberation" (4). Both Arvay and Janie are marginal characters. They have been double-marginalized and double-exploited. Janie is an Afro-American, in addition to being a woman. Arvay is depicted as "a Cracker" and originally a "white trash" in addition to being a woman. Hurston was always against submission to dominance personally. She was marginal in her era though being influential, humorous and loving as a consequence of not following the prevalent Black literary tradition of her era that was preempted by her distinguished male counterparts (Lyle 24).

However, Hurston has been immensely criticized for writing *Seraph on the Suwanee*. The main reason of this wide disapproval is portraying white main characters unlike her prior novels. In an article named "Woman Half in Shadow," which appears in *I Love Myself When I Am Laughing... & Then Again When I Am Looking Mean and Impressive: A Zora Neale Hurston Reader*, Mary Helen Washington, a black literature critic thinks of *Seraph on the Suwanee* as an evidence of Hurston's "abandoning the source of her unique esthetic-the black cultural tradition" (Hurston, Walker 21) and calls it an "awkward and contrived novel, as vacuous as a soap opera" (Hurston, Walker 7-25). Bernard Bell does not include *Seraph on the Suwanee* in his *African American novel* because he thought that it "is neither comic, nor folkloristic, nor about blacks" (128). Even Alice Walker who is obviously Hurston's most eminent fan, in *I Love Myself When I Am Laughing & Then Again When I Am Looking Mean And Impressive: A Zora Neale Hurston Reader* declares Hurston's last novel as "reactionary, static, shockingly misguided and timid" in addition to being a story "which is not even about black people, which is no crime, but is about white people for whom it is impossible to care" (xvi). In contrast with Mary Helen Washington, Alice Walker and Bernard Bell, some Hurston scholars such as Tate attempted to proclaim *Seraph on the Suwanee* as influential due to its "compelling investigations of female desire and racialized culture" (Cited in Bloom 144). The researcher also thinks that Hurston's *Seraph on the Suwanee* is influential in women's studies because it projects the life of a woman, as well as her unconscious, body and sensuality, whether Black or white. Moreover, Hurston mentioned in her *Dust Tracks on a Road* that she would like to examine "what makes a man or a woman do such-and- so, regardless of his color" (151). In another situation Hurston writes: "I belong to no race nor time. I am the eternal feminine with its strings of beads" (Kaplan, *Zora Neale Hurston: A Life in Letters* 58). In the researcher's point of view both of the selected works try to portray femininity as a universal concept whether white or black. Hurston's portrayal of "woman" agrees with Cixous's definition of "woman," who in her point of view, is "in her inevitable struggle against conventional man" (*Signs* Vol.1 No.4 875). This woman is, according to Cixous, "a universal woman subject who must bring women to their senses and to their meaning in history" (*Signs* 875-6). Cixous also invites women to "put [themselves] in to writing" (*Signs* 875). Cixous announces her invitation in "The Laugh of the Medusa" to all women regardless of their skin color in the thesis's point of view.

> I shall speak about women's writing: about *what it will do*. Woman must write her self: must write about women and bring women to writing, from which they have been driven away as violently as from their bodies-for the same reasons, by the same law, with the same fatal goal. Woman must put herself into the text-as into the world and into history-by her own movement. (*Signs* vol.1 No.4 875)

Both of the selected novels depict powerful female characters that reside in a patriarchal culture. According to Timothy Lyle, a Hurston researcher, "Unlike other writers on the left side of the movement, Hurston bravely delivers fiction that centers around [sic] strong-willed, empowered women who rise up against struggles of [sic] oppression, possession, and physical abuse in a male-dominated society" (3). Lyle writes: "In *Their Eyes Were Watching God*, "Sweat," and *Seraph on the Suwanee*, Hurston takes the reader on a journey with her female protagonist, raising issues of gender roles in the nineteenth and early twentieth century, only to deconstruct or solidify those roles by the end of the character's journey" (3).

The Arvay of *Seraph on the Suwanee* is passive but to her contrary Jim is active. Their characters are designed just according to the binary model of "activity/passivity" that is mentioned in Cixous's essay: "Sorties". Activity is almost always attributed to the masculine while passivity to the feminine. It proves Cixous's argument that mentions the entire patriarchal binary couples end in the "Man/Woman." Arvay is implied as a thoughtless character by Jim and he thinks that she is just suitable for homemaking and mothering.

122

Besides, she acts rather instinctual. By contrast, this is Jim who concentrates on everything from home and hearth to work, economy and finance. Therefore, the other binary opposition "Culture/Nature" seems to fit Jim and Arvay. Arvay's introduction as a sensitive character that understands and judges every issue intuitionally and quite instinctually recurs through the first three-quarters of the novel. But Jim is displayed as quite the opposite. He considers every issue carefully. Earl's case exposes their opposition very deliberately. Earl is a handicapped child whose symptoms of abnormality increase as he grows older though his appearance shades them away. He completely gets insane whenever he sees a girl particularly Lucy Ann Corregio, the neighbor's daughter. This problem persuades Jim to consider sending him to a mental institution which makes Arvay go crazy. Thus they quarrel:

JIM. "Now, don't ask me no dumb questions like that, honey. He's liable to hurt himself." And he stroked the wrist of her injured hand.
JIM. "He'll do harm to other folks. We ought not to risk it. No later than sunrise in the morning, we ought to take steps to put the boy away."
ARVAY. "You set there and think that I'm a'going to agree to a thing like that?" And Arvay took her hand away angrily.
ARVAY. "Putting my child in some crazy house? Nothing much wrong with Earl. He was all right, and you know it, until you fetched them furriners here on the place. They must have some different scent from regular folks and it maked Earl sick in some way or another. All you got to do is to get rid of 'em; Earl will be alright."
JIM. "No, Arvay, you're ever so wrong about that. Something about one or the other of those girls has woke up something in the boy. They didn't put it there, though. It's been there all along. You see the boy can't control himself, and we had better take things in time."(Hurston, *Seraph* 124-125)

This harsh conversation goes on until Arvay's family origin is blamed for Earl's problems. Arvay is criticized for not looking at this matter in a logical manner. Jim also oppresses Arvay by blaming her family as the cause of Earl's problems when he tells her: "'I don't hold *you* responsible for this condition. It come through your father's folks, but you didn't have nothing to do with that. I'm trying to be fair about it all I know how, but look like you won't try to meet me at all'" (Hurston, *Seraph* 127). Quite like Logan Killicks who blames Janie for what she cannot choose herself, Jim Meserve criticizes Arvay for her family. Arvay replies:

> I know that you been had it in you to say all the time. I been looking for you to puke it up long time ago. What you stay with me for, I don't know, because I know so well that you don't think I got no sense, and my folks don't amount to a hill of beans in your sight. You come from big high muck-de-mucks, and we ain't nothing but piney-woods Crackers and poor white trash. Even niggers is better than we is, according to your kind.... All I'm good for is to lay up in the bed with you and satisfy your feelings and do around here for you. Naw, I'll never give my consent for Earl to be put away. Never so long my head is warm. Earl is always wrong because he's like my folks. 'Tain't never nothing wrong with Angeline and Kenny because they take after your side. But I'm here to tell you that I'll wade in blood to knees for him. He's not going to be put away. (Hurston, *Seraph* 127)

The dichotomy "Head/Heart" is representative of Jim's logicality versus Arvay's emotionality. Another sign of Arvay's emotionality is being in love with Carl Middleton. But everything goes upside down and Carl marries Arvay's sister, Larraine. The narrator recounts that: "Even with 'Rain married to Middleton, Arvay could not bring herself to feel that her instincts had deceived her. Ah, no! There had been a mistake somewhere. Maybe even at the bottom of Carl's sudden marriage with Larraine" (Hurston, *Seraph*11). After being courted and proposed marriage by Jim Meserve, Arvay suspends her judgment as a result of her doubtfulness about marriage. Jim's answer is chauvinistic but notable:

> Women folks don't have no mind to make up nohow. They wasn't made for that. Lady folks were just made to laugh and act loving and kind and have a good man to do for them all he's able, and have him as many boy-children as he figgers he'd like to have, and make him so happy that he's willing to work and fetch in every dad-blamed thing that his wife thinks she would like to have. That's what women are made for. (Hurston, *Seraph*25)

This is quite like John Ruskin's view about the roles of women, men and their responsibilities as cited in Eagleton's *Working With Feminist Criticism* which is a deliberate portrait of binary oppositions and equals to Jim's view who believes that men possess defensive and active power and they are creators, doers and discoverers and speculators whereas women do not have the power for war but for ruling and "sweet ordering". Ruskin believes that a woman's main duty is to praise her husband who puts himself into trouble to protect her wife in his house from danger and terror (149). Ruskin's viewpoints seem to be planted in Jim's mind who "had just as good as excused the woman he married from all worry and bother" (Hurston, *Seraph* 35) and asks Arvay:

> Love and marry me and sleep with me. That is all I need you for. Your brains are not sufficient to help me with my work; you can't think with me. Let's get this thing straight in the beginning. Putting your head on the same pillow with mine is not the same thing as mingling your brains with mine any more than crying when I cry is giving you the power to feel my sorrow. You can feel my sympathy but not my sorrow. (Hurston, *Seraph* 36-37)

This makes Arvay wonder how "simple" are expectations of Jim of his future life, though she is happy that she can do all that Jim wants (Hurston, *Seraph* 36).

Joe Starks can be accused of male-chauvinism and patriarchal thinking more than Jim. He prohibits Janie from expressing her thoughts publicly and always denigrates her for every little mistake that she makes in the presence of folks. Once in the store he states: "'Somebody got to think for women and chillun and chickens and cows. I god, they don't think none theirselves'" (Hurston, *Their Eyes*71). When Janie protests and holds that women think as well as men do, he replies: "'Aw naw they don't. They just think they's thinkin'. When Ah see one thing Ah understands ten. You see ten things and don't understand one'" (Hurston, *Their Eyes*71). It will be astonishing to think that even the lovable Tea Cake is not deprived of chauvinism either (King 56). Although Tea Cake is Janie's only husband who provides her the freedom that she deserves, he is not an exception to this patriarchal dominance! He considers himself the only breadwinner and financial sponsor of hearth and home. He tells Janie: "Ah need no assistance tuh help me feed mah woman. From now on, you gointuh eat whutever mah money can buy yuh and wear de same. When Ah ain't got nothin' you don't git nothing" (Hurston, *Their Eyes* 128)

The roles that Janie's husbands demand her to perform are other kinds of oppressions imposed on her. Logan Killicks expects Janie to chop the wood, work on the field and help him around in the barn (Hurston, *Their Eyes* 26). Joe Starks does not have such expectations; on the contrary he declares that: "Ah wants to make a wife outa you" (Hurston, *Their Eyes* 29). By means of this declaration, Joe Starks reveals his intention of imposing certain reproductive roles on Janie. Both of the inflicted roles are among different versions of gender exploitation, hence they are destructive and have to be dismantled.

The other dual opposition according to Cixous's "Sorties" is "High/Low." It is noticeable in *Seraph on the Suwanee* and also in *Their Eyes Were Watching God*. Arvay is introduced as a Floridian "Cracker" and "white trash" in *Seraph on the Suwanee* and part of the people who "are born in teppentime, live all their lives in it, and die and go to their graves smelling of teppentime" (Hurston, *Seraph* 8). But Jim is originally from "upon the Alabama River" and his ancestors were landowners (Hurston, *Seraph* 7). In *Their Eyes Were Watching God*, this binary opposition is represented in its economical point. Logan has got a land of sixty acres while Janie is a sixteen or seventeen years old young woman with no property. Logan throws it into her face and blames her for being grown up in white people's house. Joe Starks is much more proud of his wealth. Therefore, Janie's first two husbands could be considered as "High" because they are men in addition to owning the property that Janie is a portion of it. But Janie is a woman and does not own anything of her own. There is an irony here that both Joe Starks and Logan Killicks do not have any children to inherit their property and lands. This conveys their fruitless result of quest for gaining property.

126

In the structure of the Meserve family, Arvay seems to be deprived of a notable place. She and her abnormal child are at the bottom of family hierarchy. Arvay Henson is a Cracker and his son Earl is said to resemble her own family. Earl is considered to look like Arvay's uncle Chester who has seldom been addressed in family conversations (Hurston, *Seraph* 68). On the other hand, Jim, Angeline and Kenny are regarded as Meserves and seem to share the same blood (Hurston, *Seraph* 199). The thought that she is ignored by her family accompanies Arvay lifelong. During their girlhood, it was Larraine who is preferred both at home and in town because she is talkative, energetic, busty and lusty in contrast to Arvay is exactly the opposite (Hurston, *Seraph* 6-9). A disregarding act that was imposed to Arvay is that Angie; her daughter marries without Arvay's permission. However, Jim is well informed about it because Angie is sixteen and he has to pass his consent as her father (Hurston, *Seraph* 186-199). This state of being unacknowledged and ignored happens during the soccer game and Kenny's performance again. Felicia Corregio is her son's date and she is not informed in advance. Jim has provided for Felicia's presence, dance ceremony and all her clothes (Hurston, *Seraph* 206-208). Arvay's husband does not consult Arvay when he moves the Corregio family to the grove either (Hurston, *Seraph* 119-120) and buys a boat to go to the sea to follow the shrimping business with Alfredo Corregio (Hurston, *Seraph* 193). Cixous discusses about a woman who is trapped and ignored in the family structure in this way:

> Whenever it is a question of woman, when one examines kinship structures, when a family model is brought into play. In fact, as soon as the question of ontology raises its head, as soon as one asks oneself "what is it?," as soon as there is intended meaning. Intention: desire, authority-examine them and you are led right back . . . to the father. It is even possible not to notice that there is no place whatsoever for woman in the calculations. . . . Either woman is passive or she does not exist. *(Cixous, Clément 64)*

Janie is also victimized by family kinship structures and hierarchies. Nanny, her grandmother who looks after her is the authority at home. Janie is not allowed to make a decision for her future. Nanny makes Janie marry much older man at the age of sixteen because she thinks that Janie is becoming a woman and after all a woman. As a result, she considers making her marry Logan Killicks to receive protection from him. Janie cannot reveal her dreams of love and marriage to Nanny. She has no other way than to consent (Hurston, *Their Eyes*12-17). Not almost one year after their marriage, Logan stops "talking in rhymes to her" and starts coercing her to work on the barn and chop the wood (Hurston, *Their Eyes* 26). He goes further to buy a mule for Janie to plow on the farm without thinking if she can suffer this physical burden or not (Hurston, *Their Eyes* 26-7). Joe Starks goes even farther than that. He has big plans in his head and is very ambitious. He wants to be the "big voice" in his own words (Hurston, *Their Eyes* 28). He regards Janie as his doll, a household woman and a shop assistant who take his orders. He never listens to Janie's thoughts and feelings and prohibits Janie from taking part in the community's gatherings and discussions. Even Janie's ever loving and unconventional Tea Cake can be accused of negligence in consulting Janie. He takes Janie's money without any acknowledgement, goes to the town, spends some of the money on his friend's newly born baby, then goes to Callahan and gives a free "big macaroni supper" to all of his friends and acquaintances (Hurston, *Their Eyes* 122). When Tea Cake recounts Janie what he has done she becomes absolutely sad and infuriated that Tea Cake did not take her with him. When Tea Cake asks her if she would go with him to the party she replies: "'Sho Ah would. Ah Laks fun just as good as you do'" (Hurston, *Their Eyes* 121). Tea Cake describes that the people who were invited to the party are not tidy and he was worried if their sight would irritate Janie, she says: "Looka heah, Tea Cake, if you ever go off from me and have a good time lak that and then come back heah tellin' me how nice Ah is, Ah specks to kill yuh dead. Heah me?" (Hurston, *Their Eyes* 121)

Hitherto, the conversations and activities that are replete with binary oppositions and hierarchical matters have been represented. Henceforth, the aim of this research is to investigate whether these patriarchal binary oppositions, hierarchies and oppressions are dismantled within the discussed novels. How and in which ways does this subversion happen?

The art of Hurston is that she does not deprive her characters of her gifts. Her characters are almost combinations of vices and virtues. However, a number of them become sarcastic. It is true that Jim is chauvinist and ambitious as much as Joe Starks but he is imbued with the gift of being as sweet as Tea Cake. Even Tea Cake has a completely round, organic and natural personality, therefore he has some flaws as well (King 54). Joe Starks with his immense pride and arrogance becomes the very object of pity particularly when Janie ridicules his impotency in the store (Hurston, *Their Eyes*79). If Janie is faced with miseries, she is achieves the highest degree of happiness in the end. Similarly Arvay's deficiencies are compensated with more notable graces. The stories are narrated very sagaciously. Though the narrator is the omniscient point of view, she does not have predilection for a certain character and entrusts it in the hands of the reader to decide whether they are wrong or right.

In *Seraph on the Suwanee,* Larraine's higher position in family and town is darkened by her aging in addition to Arvay's better marriage. It is destined for Arvay to have a better choice and therefore a better life mostly in its financial mode. Larraine's appearance is undermined as she grows older whereas Arvay remains pretty and fit. Arvay's husband works well and spends on her quite well. Whereas Larraine is poor as the result of her husband being dismissed of his job at Day Spring church, Arvay's husband and children are handsome and good-looking, whereas Carl becomes a "soiled, heavy-set man" and their children were "mule-faced" (Hurston, *Seraph* 133,275-6). Thereupon the opposition between Larrain and Arvay that is presented at the beginning of the story is reversed in this manner.

An urgent factor to be analyzed in *Seraph on the Suwanee* is Arvay's character. She is implied as a weak, hesitant and neurotic character by some readers. However the fact is that she refuses to be submissive to Jim. At the outset, she resists Jim several times and does not consent to marriage and reverses her judgment. Jim courts Arvay which is a sign of his patriarchal attitudes. Jones argues: "In his courtship rituals with Arvay, he shows a level of power and possession over her by escorting her to and from church" (155). Jim tries to attract her attention but she always ignores him deliberately though she likes him. Her procrastination and resistance toward his power rises to a level that worries the robust and confident Jim. Jim usually tries to solve his problems but one day he thinks that he wants to engage himself in something but after a while he contemplates on his situation and finds out that he is not sure that was he wanted, but he cannot help himself. He thinks with himself: "What was the matter with his engagement? He felt as if he had grabbed hold of a running man by the coat, and the man had run off, leaving him holding the empty jacket" (Hurston, *Seraph*43). The running man that he grabs hold of is the simile of Arvay who leaves Jim astray by her hesitation and resistance and preserves for him just the feeling of courtship by balking the definite answer of marriage.

When Arvay is informed that her mother has been sick, she goes to Sawley (Hurston, *Seraph* 271). Jim left home completely ahead of her telling Arvay if she wants to live with him; she has to go after him to let him know in at most a year time. Arvay that is proud on the one hand and doubtful if Jim would accept her on the other hand becomes happy to take refuge in her mother's house that seems like a heaven to her in this situation. Arvay's mother dies; thereupon she accepts the responsibility of her burial and funeral willingly. Thereafter, she begins to consider a reformation as well as contemplation upon her self and her life which resulted in her self-revelation. It can be assumed that Arvay's dependency on Jim, the impossibility of taking a challenging responsibility or going alone on a journey, being involved with the housework and children, lack of social connection with the community, separation from her mother and her roots prevented her from meditation and thus self-realization previously.

The power that Jim has over Arvay upsets her and makes her submissive to him but there are some occasions that Arvay feels her power over Jim. Arvay is very worried about the way Joe has influence on her husband. When Arvay persuades Jim to move Joe Kelsey and his family away from the grove she becomes very delighted secretly (Hurston, *Seraph* 117). Another time, she convinces Jim that Joe and his children can have a bad influence on their children, hence they have to leave there. Jim has no other way than submit to her. As a consequence "Arvay had[sic] a great feeling of power and victory. As much as Jim thought[sic] of Joe, she had[sic] more power of her husband than Joe had[sic]" (Hurston, *Seraph* 113).

It is helpful to examine the customary gender roles that are challenged within the novels. Nearly the end of *Seraph on the Suwanee* Arvay goes after Jim to the coast. She surprisingly expresses her excitement to go on fishing and shrimping trip with Jim. It is not possible at first, since she wears a dress and sandals. Jim and Arvay go uptown and buy a pair of blue jeans, two blue shirts and tall rubber boots for Arvay to change her clothes (Hurston, *Seraph* 323). Arvay who has been in the kitchen for all her life has now changed in male fishermen's clothes to go with a group of fishermen on the board. In this way she challenges her former roles.

The idea of being an obedient wife who satisfies the needs of her husband has dominant during Hurston's literary era. Hurston is not that kind of woman who obeys the patriarchal rules of her male-dominated society. She is a unique woman of her kind who has never submitted to the proper notions of marriage for the sake of her literary career and

131

anthropological studies. What Lyle writes about a "female" personality in the literature of early twentieth century is that:

> The female character either transcends or succumbs to the principles prescribed by the "cult of true womanhood," a concept that serves as a prevailing trope for scholars and critics to describe conventional gender roles of the nineteenth and twentieth century. The "cult of true womanhood" expects a woman to adhere to the four cardinal virtues of purity, piety, domesticity, and submission (Lyle 4).

In *Seraph on the Suwanee,* Hurston is scorning the notion of true womanhood that became fashionable in her era particularly, the first years after the Second World War by means of which white women have been expected to behave in a bourgeois mode. The cult of true womanhood suggests two oppositional poles. At the privileged pole of the opposition is the middle class white woman, who adheres to the rules and regulations of this culture while the subordinate pole suggests the working class, black or lower class woman who is either deprived of these virtues or tries to subvert them. By creating characters such as Janie, a free black woman in search of fulfillment and integrity and the resisting Arvay who is originally a poor cracker but turns to a be a middle class woman due to her husband's economic success, Hurston is undermining this capitalist as well as patriarchal notion.

The other gender role that is challenged in *Seraph on the Suwanee* is Arvay and Jim's adoption of new gender roles other than their being husband and wife. Their roles get the shape of mother and son mainly at the end. They feel well that she likes to take care of Jim and the young fishermen who act like little boys (Hurston, *Seraph* 341). After a long and challenging discussion, Jim asks Arvay to hug him and trembles as a child who wants to resist crying, "like a little boy who had fled in out of the dark to the comfort of his mother" (Hurston, *Seraph* 349).When Jim falls asleep in Arvay's arms, she wonders with herself:

Jim was not the over-powering general that she had took him for. Oh, he had that way with other folks and other things. No matter of doubt about it. From a teppentime shack to his own fleet on the ocean was a long, long road to travel. But that was the outside Jim. Inside he was nothing but a little boy to take care of, and he hungered for her hovering. Look at him now! Snuggled down and clutching onto her like Kenny when he wore diapers. Arvay felt like a swelling to protect and comfort Jim that tears came up in her eyes. So helpless sleeping therein her arms and trusting himself to her. *(Hurston, Seraph 351)*

In this text the hierarchical power between man and woman is reversed, as well. Now it is the woman that is more powerful than man and it is man who seeks protection in woman. Before the previously mentioned scene of Arvay and Jim's mother/son role there is another scene that presents brilliantly Jim's fear of separation of which Arvay has not been aware of before. She understands it when Jim tries to catch Arvay in a struggling manner.

Jim, Jim Meserve, Lord, had his doubts about holding hers as she had hers about him. She was not the only one who had trembled. All these years and time, Jim had been feeling his way towards her as she had been towards him. This was a wonderful and powerful thing to know, but she must not let him know what she had perceived. Arvay trembled visibly and looked up innocently afraid and scared at Jim. But one time in her life, she wanted to fully express herself in words and let him know how she had improved and changed. *(Hurston, Seraph 348)*

Janie, however, takes more noticeable measures than Arvay. When she makes sure that marriage does not make love, she does not like Logan and he does not talk in rhymes to her any more, she gives a reading to Joe Starks (Jody) who reminds her of the "Horizon" (King 53). She consents on Jody because "he spoke of change and chance" (Hurston, *Their Eyes* 29). Therefore, she considers leaving Logan. Upon facing with Logan's perpetual commands and his contempt of "her mamma, her grandma and her feelings" which she could not do anything about them, she eloped with Jody (Hurston, *Their Eyes* 32). As Hurston depicts in her masterpiece, Logan Killicks expects Janie to chop the wood, work on the field and help him around in the barn (26). Joe Starks did not have such expectations; on the contrary he declared that: "Ah wants to make a wife outa you" (29). Both of these expected gender roles are considered as types of sexual exploitation and thus destructive to a woman. Janie's resistance against Jody's patriarchy happens temporarily. They are mainly retorts to Jody's containments. As they are mostly related to Janie's gaining voice and speaking her self, they are investigated in "Voice" section. Certainly, Janie does not utter herself deliberately up to Joe Starks's death, like Arvay who does not express herself up to the end of the novel (Hurston, *Their Eyes*84-7). The big resolution of the novel in the researcher's point of view is the death of Joe Starks; Janie's pompous, arrogant and chauvinistic husband. By his death, Janie is released from a suffocating patriarchal power. She continues to protest against Jody even after his death. She goes and burns all of her head rags that Jody forces her to tie on her head and releases her plentiful hair immediately after his death (Hurston, *Their Eyes* 89). The head kerchiefs are symbols of Jody's patriarchal confinement that Janie dismantles them at last.

When Joe Starks dies, everybody threatens Janie of the risks of widowhood. She has been told over and over that "Uh woman by herself is uh pitiful thing" and they are in need of men's assistance (Hurston, *Their Eyes* 90). She is told: "You'se too young uh 'oman tuh stay single, and you'se too pretty for de mens tuh leave yuh alone. You'se bound tuh marry"(91). Most of the people who warn her consider for her beauty and property. There are many men who admire, want and respect her in a way as if she is the "Empress of Japan" but some regard it as unsuitable to reveal their longing because she is Joe Starks's widow (93). It can be assumed that they regard her as Joe Starks's property even after his death.

By her unconventional marriage to Tea Cake, Janie not only protests against Nanny who died many years ago but also she challenges the community's beliefs on a traditional marriage. Nanny's viewpoints that are deeply rooted in her unconscious were then being undermined. Tea Cake is extremely black, penniless and uninhibited. The people of Eatonville believe that she might "class off" and get married to a man of her same rank because he is Mayor Starks's widow anyway. She undermines this issue as well. After getting married to Tea Cake, she continues associating with every kind of people that might be considered lower than her and hereby opposes Jody's idea that she had to class off (Hurston, *Their Eyes* 112).

There are some gender roles and conventions that are undermined in *Their Eyes Were Watching God* which take place after Tea Cake and Janie's marriage. The first of which is playing checkers. Tea Cake asks her to play checkers with him and teaches her how to do it when she tells him that she does not know how to play. It is undoubtedly pleasing for her that somebody asks her to play and regards it as "natural for her to play" (Hurston, *Their Eyes* 96). In spite of their being surprised at Janie playing checkers, they like it (Hurston, *Their Eyes* 101). Janie's next unusual deed is go fishing at night. The narrator says: "It was so crazy digging worms by lamp light and setting out for Lake Sabelia after midnight that she felt like a child breaking rules. That's what made Janie like it. They caught two or three and got home just before day" (102). It seems to Janie that she is breaking the conventional rules by going fishing at night for the first time in her life.

What people of Eatonville react to severely is that Janie ceases to mourn for her dead husband and changes into colorful clothes. She wears new dresses and different hairstyles. Even her close friend Phoeby objects to her. She replies Phoeby: "Ah ain't grievin' so why do Ah hafta mourn? Tea Cake loves me in blue, so Ah wears it. Jody ain't never in his life picked out no color for me. De world picked out black and white for mournin', Joe didn't. So Ah wasn't wearin' it for him. Ah was wearin' it for de rest of y'all" (Hurston, *Their Eyes* 113). Janie's arguments imply that the societal rules and conventional beliefs of people that make a person behave in a specific way. However, Janie determines to live her own life and be her own self. Janie's firm decision "will tear her away from the superegoized structure in which she has always occupied the place reserved for the guilty" (Cixous, *Signs* vol.1 No.4 880). Janie tends to wear what satisfies her taste without taking into notice what different subjects of patriarchal structure expect her to do.

Janie's most influential activity is her efforts in learning to shoot. Thanks to Tea Cake, Janie has learnt how to handle a gun. They practice it every day while they have been on the muck. Tea Cake has trained Janie how to shoot pistol, shot gun and rifle. They hunt animals and even one night they go to hunt alligators (Hurston, *Their Eyes* 131). Three weeks after the hurricane they buy a pistol and a rifle and practice. Janie is better than Tea Cake in handling the rifle. This makes Tea Cake jealous but proud of her. Volleying with gun is a practice usually associated with men and a symbol of masculinity. By exploiting them, Janie enters the masculine territory and has managed to use male symbol of power and has thus reversed another gender role as well as patriarchal hierarchy.

When Janie and Tea Cake are on the muck, working on the fields and in quarters, a teenage girl named Nunkie flirts with Tea Cake and attracts his attentions. These flirtations lasted for three weeks when Janie realizes that Tea Cake and Nunkie are disappeared. She follows and finds them. She makes an unsuccessful attempt to catch the girl and then goes home while Tea Cake follows her. That day they fight and Janie beats Tea Cake as this event can reveal Tea Cake's infidelity toward Janie (King 56). If there is no hint of infidelity there has been no jealousy. Infidelity is another form of oppression. It is caused by Tea Cake's chauvinism (King 56). It is interesting that Hurston herself does not try to reveal the meaning clearly. Hurston moves the reader into a language play and this is the reader who must learn if Tea Cake has had an affair with Nunkie or not. The reader is convinced that Tea Cake has flirted with Nunkie though stocked in Hurston's wordplay. Moreover, the following passages represent the deferral of meaning which is a hint of deconstructionist capability of Hurston's text.

> JANIE. "Ah b'lieve you been messin' round her!" she panted furiously.
> TEA CAKE. "No sich uh thing!" Tea Cake retorted.
> JANIE. "Ah b'lieve yuh did."
> TEA CAKE. "Don't keer how big uh lie get old, somebody kin b'lieve it!"
> They fought on. "You done hurt mah heart, now you come wid uh lie tuh bruise mah ears! Turn go mah hands!" Janie seethed. But Tea Cake never let go. They wresteld on until they were doped with their own fumes and emanations; till their clothes had been torn away; till he hurled her to the floor and held her there . . . The Next morning Janie asked like a woman, "You still love ole Nunkie?"
> TEA CAKE. "Naw, never did, and you know it too. Ah didn't want her."
> JANIE. "Yeah, you did." She didn't say this because she believed it.
> She wanted to hear his denial. She had to crow over the fallen Nunkie.
> (Hurston, *Their Eyes* 138)

An example of gender role reversal is Mrs. and Mr. Turner. Mrs. Turner is proud of her white features, but she possesses masculine mood. At the night that Tea Cake and other guys set up a fight in her restaurant then leave there messy with her hand broken and go away, "she saw her husband siting over there in the corner with his boney legs all crossed up smoking his pipe" (Hurston, *Their Eyes* 152). Then she tells her husband: "What kinda man is *you*, Turner? You see dese no count niggers come in heah and break up mah place! How kin you set and see yo' wife all trompled on? You ain't no kinda man at all. You seen dat Tea Cake shove me down! You ain't raised yo' hand tuh do nothin' about it." (Hurston, *Their Eyes* 152)

Mrs. Turner is used to visit Janie because she likes her "coffee and cream complexion." She hates niggers, their color, habits and manners though she is a black herself. She curses Negroes to a high extent. She even suggests Janie to see her brother because she thinks that they can make up well. Tea Cake is angry and afraid of her meddling in their life so he decides to warn her husband not to let her come to their house. Mr. Turner's reaction is to say:

""Mah wife takes time fuh whatever she wants tuh do. Real strong headed dat way. Yes indeed." He laughed a high lungless laugh. "De chillun don't keep her in no mo' so she visits when she chooses"" (Hurston, *Their Eyes* 144). Mr. Turner's words imply that he has not such a power over her wife.

Tea Cake's being murdered by Janie nearly at the end of the story is another act of resistance toward male authority and thus releasing from it. However, it is done unintentionally, unconsciously and maybe instinctually. Janie volleys Tea Cake to secure herself from being killed by the rabid Tea Cake (Hurston, *Their Eyes*184). This final sorrowful measure helps her to reach complete independency and ultimate self-revelation.

Although *Seraph on the Suwanee* has been recognized as an unsuccessful attempt by an Afro-American artist to influence a white readership, Hurston regards the novel as an attempt to end the ridiculous notion that black artists are only allowed to write about the experiences of black people (Cited in Lyle 16). According to Lyle, Hurston represents the "cult of true womanhood" as a way of living for a woman and puts black women in similar position with white women in a common strife for equality and identity in a male-dominated world. Moreover, by displaying the responsibilities of marriage and motherhood as patriarchal activities and examining its effects on the mind and body of a middle-class white woman, Hurston shows in what ways woman's endeavor goes beyond both race and class limits (Lyle 16).

According to Claudia Tate, Hurston is deconstructing the notion of "romantic love" in patriarchal narratives by means of playing jokes on "passive female desire," "class" and "race" that are highly idealized throughout the white culture. Like Cixous who tries to dismantle Freudian phallogocentric ideas about female desire and its interconnection with passivity, Hurston has tried to criticize "passive female desire, indeed female masochism" in *Seraph on the Suwanee* (Cited in Bloom 144).

Though Hurston seems to apply white characters in *Seraph on the Suwanee*, she is deconstructing the binary opposition White/Black by representing Jim as a "Black Irish" (Hurston, *Seraph* 7). According to David R. Roediger, Jim's label refers to a mixed white and black blood, resulting from the Irish "intermixing with shipwrecked slaves" (Cited in Bloom 4). Hurston has also identified the white-faced Arvay and Jim with "black voices", because they speak in the black vernacular of Eatonville, using their idioms in Tate's point of view (Cited in Bloom 148). The other situation where Hurston dismantles the hierarchy White/Black is where the white protagonists of the novel seek assistance from the black characters. When Jim cannot understand whether Arvay loves him or not, he asks for some advice from Joe Kelsey; his pet Negro (Hurston, *Seraph* 45-6). Similarly, Arvay determines to save her marriage by requesting Joe Kelsey and his wife to take her to the coast (Hurston, *Seraph* 313).

There are hints of mutual cooperation and friendship between the nonwhite and whites within *Seraph on the Suwanee*. In addition to the close relationship between the Meserve family and the Kelsey family, some boats on the coast are consisted of "mixed crews" while the white and the Negroes are friendly together (Hurston, *Seraph* 323). When Kenny Meserve, the last child of the family leaves university to work with a music band in New York, Joe Kelsey goes to see him. Arvay pleads him to "stand by him" and persuades Kenny to come home with him (Hurston, *Seraph* 252). Furthermore, she confesses that she is happy that Kenny appreciates him (Hurston, *Seraph* 251). In fact, this is Joe who has taught Kenny to play the guitar though Kenny has inherited the talent from her mother (Hurston, *Seraph* 159 &250). Later, Kenny cultivates the black folk music and mixes it with other genres and is the first white musician who performs this new genre of mixed black music (Hurston, *Seraph* 236). Hereby Hurston challenges Jim Crow's segregationist rules that have been dominant in that era and have tried to separate white and black people.

As a whole, *Seraph on the Suwanee* is capable to be read as a deconstruction of racial binary oppositions. It acts like a revolutionary text that criticizes bourgeoisie classifications and racial restrictions. According to Claudia Tate:

> Like the "carnivalized" body that Bakhtin described, the white bodies of *Seraph's* protagonists, with their black speaking voices, are not closed, complete, defined, or totalized social entities. Since Arvay and Jim repeatedly transgress the boundaries of their presumed racial categories, they are neither entirely white nor black. (Cited in Bloom153)

The rattlesnake and the gun are symbols of masculinity and male power (Lyle 15). Tea Cake is a marksman and he instructs Janie how to shoot. But Janie; his pupil turns out to be better than him in shooting. At the end, Tea Cake is killed by Janie's shooting ironically (Hurston, *Their Eyes* 184). Thus, his power is undermined by his own symbol of power and control. Jim Meserve also approaches the border of death by rattlesnake. He is showing off his ability of handling the rattlesnake to Arvay that he is choked to death by it (Hurston, *Seraph* 253-6). These hints prove how masculine signs turn out to victimize their male counterparts.

Another arguable point about *Seraph on the Suwanee* is that Jim's perspectives and expectations of a good wife have gone under a process of change. At first he tells Arvay that "Women folks don't have no mind to make up nohow" (Hurston 35). Or he said her: "Love and marry me and sleep with me. That is all I need you for. Your brains are not sufficient to help me with my work; you can't think with me" (Hurston 36). Jim deconstructs himself when he decides to leave Arvay because he is fed up with her dumbness and told her that: "But to come right down to the fact of the matter, you and me have been never really married. Our bonds have never been consecrated. Two people ain't never married until they come to the same point of view" (266). His views on marriage have changed during these years of his married life. He does not think the way that he thought twenty-two years ago. His sentences are additionally the symptoms of his seeking dominance over Arvay's mind. But Arvay always resists and Jim cannot gain her mind as he dominates over her body.

By means of examining the novels, it is assumed that there are binary oppositions, gender roles, hierarchies and oppressions within them that have to be dismantled. As far as it has been discussed, though some critics disregard *Seraph on the Suwanee* as Hurston's weak and anti-feminist novel, it implies interesting and deconstructive points that make it evident as a scorn of white male-dominated culture as well as "the cult of true womanhood."

Throughout this chapter, the thesis has scrutinized the notions of voice and body within *Their Eyes Were Watching God* and *Seraph on the Suwanee* in addition to discovering if binary oppositions are broken or oppression is dismantled. It is presumed that there have been some imposed reproductive roles that were reversed or destroyed within both of the novels. Furthermore, the heroines have changed to powerful women up to the end of the course of novels. They are conversed to women who are aware of their latent feminine power. Moreover, they have gained their voice which is an influential weapon in order to challenge patriarchy.

The texts of Hurston convey vocal and subversive qualities in themselves. They are full of rhythm, sounds and songs that add to its vocal qualities. They are subversive because they resist revealing their meaning in a simple way in addition to Hurston's attitude to give voice to the marginal and silent individuals of society. The texts of Zora are modes of criticism of society's male-dominated rules, conventions and limitations.

CHAPTER FIVE

Conclusion

5.1. Summing Up

Throughout this chapter, the thesis is going to review what has been surveyed in the previous chapters regarding the theory and its application on the selected novels. The major ideas and notions are going to be revised again in order to sum them up. Thereafter the results of the research will be revealed. At the end, a number of suggestions of other possible readings of Zora Neale Hurston's and further fruitful approaches and studies will be introduced.

Regarding the theory, the researcher has selected Cixous's post-structuralist feminist criticism and theories to fulfill the thesis which has been investigated widely in chapter two. After presenting a preface to feminism and its history as well as an introduction of the influential figures such as Woolf, De Beauvoir, Lacan and Derrida who performed significant roles in the current of post-structuralist feminism, the thesis commenced reviewing post-structuralist feminism followed by concentrating on the French deconstructionist intellectual, Hélène Cixous and considering her theories.

Cixous speaks and writes not only for women but also men though she is addressing "woman" particularly in her essay "The Laugh of the Medusa." Cixous and her followers practice a feminine mode of writing which is called écriture féminine or "writing the body". This unique kind of writing, according to Cixous, is practiced by those subjects who are "breakers of automatisms" and "marginal characters" to which no authority can ever subjugate (*Signs* vol.1 NO.4 883). Feminine writing has some significant features that have been discussed widely. First of all, a feminine writing privileges voice (Cixous, Clément 92). It possesses other distinctive features such as openness. An open text does not signify a "simple or linear" writing even if it is "'theoretical'" or "political" (Cixous, Clément 92). Such a kind of writing does not possess a serious grammatical patterning, necessarily. Another prominent quality of a feminine writing is multiplicity of signifiers which can be gained by means of metaphor, pun and bisexuality. Another factor is "delighting in otherness" (Eagleton, *Working* 182). Other characteristics are "concern with physicality and body" in addition tocreativity (Eagleton, *Working* 182). "Patriarchal binary thought" that is constructed upon binary oppositions is another notion that Cixous is concerned with (Eagleton, *Working* 146). She seeks to study their roots in cultural systems in order to provide the means of their dismantling. Therefore, the existence of binary oppositions or other means of patriarchy such as gender roles that are constructed by society are resisted within the texts. This thesis explores the notions of multiplicity and openness in chapter three. In chapter four, the elements of body, voice, and resisting patriarchy have been investigated.

The heroines of *Their Eyes Were Watching God* and *Seraph on the Suwanee* are both the victims of patriarchy. As it is portrayed by Zora Neale Hurston in both of the novels, the female protagonists are entrapped in patriarchal contexts that prevent their independence, freedom, desired gender roles and voice from being fulfilled. Thus, Janie and Arvay; the heroines of *Their Eyes Were Watching God* and *Seraph on the Suwanee* are enfeebled to passive subjects, unable to speak as a result of their oppressors who regulate such systems.

As Hurston presents in her novel, Janie; the heroine of *Their Eyes Were Watching God* is convinced to marry a landowner who is many years older than her in order to receive protection. Logan who is her first husband forces her to work on the field. Moreover, he does not represent the romantic man of Janie's dreams. Therefore, she considers eloping with a man whom she calls Jody. Janie's Jody is promoted to the mayor of Eatonville and as a result disagrees with certain roles, gestures and restrictions on her. In addition, he deprives Janie of the chance to speak. He dies later and Janie gets emancipated from a notable oppression. This

143

time, she considers marrying to Tea Cake who is "organic," romantic and absolutely unconventional (King 56). He provides Janie the freedom to choose her favorite roles. However, he is as chauvinist as and as jealous as Joe Starks as he considers himself responsible for providing financial support and Janie obliges herself to be satisfied with this situation. Tea Cake's most chauvinistic attempt can be hitting Janie to prove his dominance over Janie to the Turner family. In fact, Tea Cake's action reassures him in "possession" (Hurston, *Their Eyes* 147). Tea Cake is attacked by a rabid dog in the hurricane, gets insane and is shot by Janie while he is attempting to kill her.

Seraph on the Suwanee presents the accounts of a resisting woman called Arvay with multitude of concerns and plural fluid identities. She consents to marry the domineering Jim and is entrapped in his confinements that oblige her to serve him. She attempts to emancipate herself from his restraints on several occasions. She does not recognize her own power and potentials until the time that she seeks revelation under the mulberry tree after her return to her mother at her death bed and taking the responsibility of her funeral. She manages to confront with Jim when she realizes her empowerment and they reconcile as its consequence. Before this reconciliation, Arvay challenges her former reproductive roles by changing into fishermen's clothes and adapting the role of a mother to Jim and other fishermen.

5.2. Findings

In the preceding section, the general current of the thesis has been discussed and the aim of the research has been revealed. There has been a brief introduction of Cixousian model of study as well as reviews of the novels and the problems that the thesis aims to solve.

According to Cixous, it is not possible to describe what a "feminine practice of writing" is because it is something that cannot be "theorized" (*Signs* vol.1 NO.4 883). However, by means of applying a number of factors, a feminine writing is capable to be produced. By inspecting these characteristics within a certain text, the reader can practice a feminine kind of reading as well as finding out whether the text that is under his/her study is a model of écriture féminine. These distinctive elements and features are: openness, multiplicity, creativity, body and "delighting in otherness" according to Mary Eagleton. In addition, deconstruction of patriarchy and bearing voice are further significant features. The researcher aims to investigate the significance of openness, multiplicity, body and voice as well as resistance toward patriarchy in Hurston's novels; *Their Eyes Were Watching God* and *Seraph on the Suwanee.*

An open text is a text that is not dominated by a repressive system. It is characterized by its fluidity and circularity. According to King, Janie narrates the story of her adventures and life "in her rural southern black vernacular" (60). Furthermore, Hazel V. Carby writes: "There are many phrases and sentences that evoke the language of Hurston's black figures in her previous work" (Hurston, *Seraph* ix). This black vernacular does not follow the pronunciation, spelling and grammatical rules of Standard English. In addition, some words are repeated in a certain sentence that adds to the circularity of the text. *Their Eyes Were Watching God* is a story that begins with an end or almost ends with the beginning; Janie enters Eatonville after about two years and the story finishes after Janie finishes the story she is telling to Phoeby and goes upstairs to sleep and remember her memories about Tea Cake. This model of beginning and ending adds to the story's quality of openness.

Metaphor and pun are among the literary figures that produce multiple signifiers and thus cause the deferment of the meaning. This is a distinctive characteristic of a post-structural text. There are numerous metaphoric elements, phrases and sentences as well as pun in both *Their Eyes Were Watching God* and *Seraph on the Suwanee* that help the thesis to prove the plurality of them. In addition, the quality of being bisexual is another factor that results in plurality. In fact, there is not much trace of bisexuality except the homoerotic desire that the reader feels when Janie tells Phoeby: "Ah don't mean to bother with tellin' 'em nothin',

Phoeby.'Tain't worth de trouble. You can tell 'em what Ah say if you wants to. Dat's just de same as me 'cause mah tongue is in mah friend's mouf" (Hurston, *Their Eyes* 6). The vision that is recognized in *Seraph on the Suwanee* is when Arvay is staring at Larraine's neck and the same night dreams it being torn away by a tiger in the jungle. This can be considered as a bisexual element within the novel which adds to the plural identities of Arvay. According to Jones, Arvay's character is evidently "the most striking example of a person in search of identity, as her situation constantly changes throughout the novel" (153-4). It suggests the Kristevan notion of "subject in process." Janie's fluidity of class, desires and economic status provides a similar plural and open space within the novel. The multiplicity of their identities and their attempts in order to actualize them is provided and projected by means of certain metaphors. Janie and Arvay's situation reminds of Cixous's statements where she argues: "The subject is a non-closed mixed of self/s and other" as well as a "subject is at least a thousand people" (Sellers xviii).

A substantial characteristic of a post-structuralist text is its attempt to adapt the notions of body and corporeality in order to challenge patriarchy. It can be assumed that there are multitudes of examples and excerpts within both of the novels that are abundant with erotic qualities. The most sensual passage in American literature appears in *Their Eyes Were Watching God* according to Kaplan (115). It implies Hurston's apparent commitment to allocating her works to body. The harassments that women undergo are depicted in a metaphoric manner. Nanny's indication of being assaulted by her master is revealed in euphemism. *Seraph on the Suwanee*, similar to *Their Eyes Were Watching God* is full of references to heroines' desires for expression, fulfillment and empowerment. Both Janie and Arvay apply their bodies as sites of resistance toward patriarchy.

Janie and Arvay, the protagonists of the selected stories, try their best to challenge patriarchy. An influential means of this resistance is their voices. Janie does not remain silent toward Nanny who pushes her to marry brother Logan Killicks, however she does not insist. She expresses her dissatisfaction and reveals her desire for a more romantic marriage although she is not successful in persuading Nanny. She also tries to rebel against Logan who aims to make her work on the field. She disobeys Logan's orders and challenges him by means of her pertinacity. She goes on until there is no other way than to escape from his house. Janie turns to silence as a result of Joe Starks's oppressions, preventions and dominance. On some occasions, she attempts to give a speech. In spite of Joe Starks's limitations, she is a good orator. However, she gains back her voice nearly after twenty years and tries to defend herself against Joe's patriarchy. Arvay is not successful in revealing the words and visions of her mind at the outset, either. Both Arvay and her husband Jim cannot have a good verbal communication. They always misunderstand each other or quarrel. But at the end of the novel, Arvay gains the ability to transfer to a good orator who can express her empowerment and shiver the roots of masculinity.

The novels make efforts in challenging patriarchy by deconstructing the societal gender constructions. Immediately after Joe's death, Janie burns all of her head rags as a sign of her rebellion against what Joe and perhaps the community imposes on her. She sits on the porch and listens to the stories just like other members of the community. Taking the mourning clothes away and marrying the poor young Tea Cake irritate the community to the most possible degree. She plays checkers on the store porch and practices activities that are forbidden for her not only as a woman but also as the mayor's wife. She goes fishing with Tea Cake at night, practices marksmanship, learns driving and goes to work on the field with poor Black workers voluntarily. By means of these activities, Janie is dismantling the rules that urge her to "class off" as the mayor's wife and widow. Tea Cake is romantic, conventional and natural; however he attempts to mark Janie as his possession. There is additionally a hint of his infidelity to which Janie confronts by means of her physical resistance. Eventually, she emancipates herself from Tea Cake's chauvinism, jealousy and possessive attitudes by shooting him in order to save herself from being killed by him. Gun is considered as a male symbol and a patriarchal tool of oppression. The ironical point of Tea Cake's murder is that it is Tea Cake who has trained Janie in marksmanship. In addition, he is killed by a male symbol of power. Thus, he is killed by his own oppression just like Joe Starks. He has always denigrated Janie verbally. Janie ceases to be silent and revenges him by applying the oppressive tool that he has always inflicted on her. She attempts to degrade him by means of castrating words and reveals her unspoken opinions about him. Moreover, Janie's body possesses a significant role in resisting conventional beliefs, the oppressing eyes and minds as the representatives of patriarchy. It is inferred that Janie attempts to undermine diverse confining rules about gender and class.

The researcher thinks that Arvay's resistance to marriage has been an attitude toward resisting male-dominance. The hysterical spasm or in Hurston's words, "fits," could be considered as her means of challenging the oppressive system similar to what Dora is reported to do by Freud as well as Cixous's *The Case Of Dora* . Her attempts to leave Jim, her negligence in helping him when he is going to be nearly choked by the rattlesnake shows her favor in removing her husband from her life and becoming emancipated. Similar to Joe Starks and Tea Cake, Jim is going to be nearly murdered by his own patriarchy because rattlesnake and snake are considered as male symbols and thus aim to point to men's power. Arvay's final action to go on the shrimping ship and putting on fisherman's clothes as well as playing the role of mother for both Jim and other fishermen on the board are considered as her attempts to challenge her former gender roles.

It was indicated that Cixous feels the femininity within writing by "a privilege of voice" (Cixous, Clément 92). The notion of voice has been mentioned during the previous discussion, to some extent. The research comes upon this conclusion that the female protagonists, who are considered as marginal, gain their voices within the stories soon or late. They try to challenge their husbands' dominance over them by means of their speech. It is as a result of gaining her voice and actualizing her feminine power that Arvay states: "I was born with all I ever needed to handle you case" (Hurston, *Seraph on the Suwanee* 347).

These are not just the characters who add to the privilege of voice within the texts but the rhythm, dialogues, conversations, monologues, songs, sermons and other elements add to this feature. Both *Their Eyes Were Watching God* and *Seraph on the Suwanee* seem to bear the requisite characteristics to celebrate voice. Both of the novels are abundant with dialogues, songs and sermons. Their diction is sometimes alliterative. Furthermore, the syntax is rhythmic and reverberating; it establishes a close connection with music and song. Music is present within the characters, the context and the text itself. Arvay plays the organ and his son Kenny starts learning the guitar since childhood, and he is so innovative that he establishes his own band as well as his own music. Tea Cake also sings and plays the guitar. However, *Their Eyes Were Watching God* is more powerful in this sense. Storytelling plays a meaningful role in the formation of the novel. Nanny narrates her story and preaches her sermon to Janie, people tell stories on the porch, Joe Starks gives sermons in the community gatherings and eventually, Janie tells her story to Phoeby. *Their Eyes Were Watching God* seems to offer stories within a story.

There are references in both of the novels that point to different things as inscription, writing and text: After Nanny narrates her story, she says Janie: "So whilst Ah was tendin' you of nights Ah said Ah'd save de text for you" (Hurston; *Their Eyes* 17). In later chapters, Hurston writes: "No matter what Jody did, she said some. She was a rut in the road. Plenty of life beneath the surface but it was kept beaten down by the wheels" (*Their Eyes* 76). These sentences are capable to refer to a multi-layered writing. They convey two layers of meanings that exist in Janie.

There are similar metaphoric sentences referring to writing in *Seraph on the Suwanee*. After their premature intimacy, Arvay thinks that "her mother might be standing there and would read her like a book" (Hurston, *Their Eyes* 54). In the mentioned excerpt, there is an indication of reading which is closely connected to writing. It conveys the textual quality of Arvay's corporeality. At the end of the novel a similar sentence is declared by both Arvay and Jim for two or three times: "I can read your writing" (Hurston, 346-7). According to Tate, this sentence means that both Arvay and Jim are able to understand each other's desires which are hidden under their actions or repressions (Cited in Bloom147).

The discussed notions in addition to the achieved conclusions would suffice to proclaim *Their Eyes Were Watching God* and *Seraph on the Suwanee* as models of écriture féminine. They bear the characteristics of being plural and open. In addition, they resist patriarchy by and large. The heroines' bodies as well as their voice are regarded as the major means to dismantle patriarchy. The texts privilege voice, put an end to the marginal protagonists' silences and resist patriarchal binary thought. There is resistance toward the conventional marriage. Moreover, Hurston is resisting the cult of traditional womanhood by portraying a rebellious heroine such as Janie. She is also scorning this notion in *Seraph on the Suwanee* via Arvay's character. These points add to the potential to be tagged as examples of feminine writing.

5.3. Suggestions for Further Research

Chapter five represents a revision of the former chapters heretofore. Based on the outcomes, it is concluded that *Their Eyes Were Watching God* and *Seraph on the Suwanee* are considered écriture feminine. In this section the thesis is exploring other possible researches that could be performed on the texts or other works by Hurston.

Zora Neale Hurston's works and particularly *Their Eyes Were Watching God* are capable to be studied under the light of different post-structuralist trends. As mentioned formerly, Virginia Heffernan writes about *Their Eyes Were Watching God* like this:

> New readers found a forceful, erotic, well-wrought story about a black woman by a black woman, and academics in newly formed African-American studies departments had particular need for it. For one reason, its narrative technique, which is heavy on free-indirect discourse, lent itself to poststructuralist analysis.
>
> (*New York Times*, March 4, 2005)

This quotation is mentioned as an evidence of the quality of the selected texts to be read by means of post-structuralist approaches.

They can be studied by means of Foucauldian approaches. The notions of sexuality or violence as well as gender can be explored within them in the light Foucault. Researchers can examine Butler's theory of gender within the texts especially in the two selected novels. Lacan's Psychoanalysis and his followers' approaches particularly Kristevan theories seem to be possible and fruitful to be worked out on Hurston's novels or short stories. Anthropology, Folklore and Cultural Studies are particularly well-known to be applied on Hurston's works. The researchers can deal with these novels or Hurston's other works by means of cultural theories of Spivak. The study of the selected novels would seem fruitful under the light of postmodernist feminism or femaleness theories. As they are the productions of an Afro-American novelist, different trends of colonialist and post-colonialist studies are helpful to be worked out on Hurston's works. Other critic that one might be successful in applying his approach is Bakhtin. In addition, different trends and theories of Marxist criticism are applicable on Hurston's texts. A researcher can read Hurston's novels and short stories by means of other feminist criticisms such as Black feminism and womanism as well as Freudian studies successfully. The presence of natural elements such as special trees, the sea, certain

151

fruits as well as the heroines' quest make archetypal readings of the selected novels possible and fruitful.

The other group of researches and theses that are possible are those which try to deal with different notions and concepts within Hurston's works. There are many glittering concepts within Hurston's works that worth conducting a research. One of these concepts and notions, in the researcher's point of view are the significance of God and religion within Hurston's works, especially within the selected works in this thesis. Storytelling is another element, the study of which will result in satisfactory results, particularly in *Their Eyes Were Watching God*. The study of love and hate within the selected novels of this research is applicable as well. Researchers can survey these two notions by means of post-structuralist feminist critics like Kristeva as well as Cixous. The thesis would like to support these suggestions by mentioning two highly impressive quotations about hate and love, one about hate and the other about love. The first one is from Cixous, and the other one is written by Hurston in *Their Eyes Were Watching God*. Cixous in *The Laugh of the Medusa* writes:

> Men have committed the greatest crime against women. Insidiously, violently, they have led them to hate women, to be their own enemies, to mobilize their immense strength against themselves, to be executants of their virile needs. They have made for women an anti-narcissism! A narcissism which loves itself only to be loved for what women haven't got! They have constructed the infamous logic of antilove. (*Signs* Vol.1 No.4 878)

Researchers can work out the post-structuralist feminism from a perspective different from what has been applied in this research. The feeling of hate happens within *Seraph on the Suwanee* as well as *Their Eyes Were Watching God* several times. They could be investigated through the lens of Cixous. Love is the opposite concept that has a significant role in both of the selected novels. Hurston's most impressing words about love appear in *Their Eyes Were Watching God* when Janie tells Phoeby:

152

"Dey gointuh make 'miration 'cause mah love didn't work lak they love, if dey ever had any. Then you must tell 'em love ain't lak uh grindstone dat's de same thing everywhere and do de same thing tuh everything it touch. Love is lak de sea. It's uh movin' thing, but still and all, it takes its shape from de shore it meets, and it's different with every shore."
(Hurston, *Their Eyes* 191)

The study of the notion of love can be fulfilled under the light of other theorists who have discussed this concept.

Hurston's works are capable to be read along with other American or Afro-American writers, both men and women in different courses of comparative studies by means of different approaches. There are many common concepts between Hurston and authors like Walker, Morrison or Maya Angelou, as Hurston is considered as the literary fore-mother of her next generations of black female writers. The works of Hurston's contemporary female authors such as Eudora Welty and Nella Larson are capable to be compared with her regarding the different aspects that are common between their works. The works of Harlem Renaissance figures such as Langston Hughes seem to be suitable to be sought in a project of comparative studies. In addition, Hurston's plays, theatrical reviews and short stories should not be neglected.

Works Cited

Alexander, Laura. "Hélène Cixous and the Rhetoric of Feminine Desire." n.d. *cornell*.<www.arts.cornell.edu/english/publications/mode/.../alexander.doc>.

Beneš, Jan. "Discourse on Sexuality in the Works of Zora Neale Hurston." *Thesis*. Masaryk University, 2011.

Bloom, Harold.ed. *Bloom's Modern Critical Views: Zora Neale Hurston*. New York: Infobase Publishing, 208.

Bernard, Patrick S. "The Cognitive Construction of Self in Hurston's *Their Eyes Were Watching God*." *Comparative Literature and Culture* 9.2 (1-14)

Bernard, W Bell. *The Afro-American Novel and Its Tradition*. Amherst: The University of Massachuset Press, 1989.

Bressler, Charles E. *Literary Criticism, An Introduction to Theory and Practice*. Fourth Edition. Upper Saddle River: Pearson Education, 2007.

Briganti, Chiara and Robert Con Davis. "Hélène Cixous." *John Hopkins Guide to Literary Theory and Criticism*. Baltimore: John Hopkins University Press, 1994.

Carby, Hazel V. "Foreword," in *Seraph on the Suwanee*. New York: Harper Perennial, 1991.

Cixous, Hélène and Catherine Clément. *The Newly Born Woman*. Trans. Betsy Wing. Vol. 24. Minneapolis: University of Minnesota Press, 1988.

Cixous, Hélène. "'Castration or Decapitation?'." Eagleton, Mary. *Feminist Literary Theory, A Reader*. Ed. Mary Eagleton.2nd Edition. Oxford: Blackwell Publishing, 2005. 322-5.

---. "The Laugh of the Medusa." *Signs* 1 (1976): 875-893

Cuddon, J. A. *The Penguin Dictionary*. London: Penguin Croup, 1998.

Daram, Mahmood and Sepideh Hozhabrsadat. "The Invisibility of I's In *Their Eyes Were Watching God*." *Internal Journal of English Literature and Culture* 3(4) (June 2012): 84-90.

"drive". Oxford Dictionaries. April 2010. Oxford Dictionaries. April 2010. Oxford University Press. 30 November 2012 <http://oxforddictionaries.com/definition/english/drive>.

Eagleton, Mary. *Working with Feminist Criticism*. Oxford: Blackwell & Wiley Publishers, 1996.

---. *Feminist Literary Theory, A Reader*. Oxford: Blackwell Publishing, 2005.

Emery, Amy Fass. "The Zombie In/ As the Text: Zora Neale Hurston's *Tell My horse*." *African American Review* 39.3 (2005): 327-366.

"Feminism." Merriam-Webster.com.Meriam-Webster,2012. Web. 2. Nov, 2012.<http://www. merriam-webster.com/dictionary/feminism?shoe=0&t=1354127787>

Gamble, Sarah. *Routledge Companion to Feminism and Postfeminism.* New York: Routledge, 2002.

Harris-Perry, Mellisa. *SisterCitizen: Shame, Stereotypes and Black Women in America.* Pennsylvania: Yale University, 2011.

Haurykiewicz, Julie A. "From Mules to Muliebrity: Speech and Silence in *Their Eyes Were Watching God.*" *The Southern Literary Journal* 29.2 (Spring, 1997): 45-60.

Heffernan, Virginia. "A Woman on a Quest, via Hurston and Oprah." *The New York Times* 4 March. 2005.

Hubbard, Dolan. ""...Ah said Ah'd save de text for you"": Recontextualizing the Sermon to Tell (Her)story in Zora Neale Hurston's Their Eyes Were Watching God." In Harold Bloom, *Zora Neale Hurston.* New York: Infobase Publishing.

Hurston, Zora Neale. *Dust Tracks on a Road.* Ed. Henry Louis Gates, JR. New York: Harper Perennial, 1996.

—. *Seraph on the Suwanee.* Ed. Henry Louis Gates,JR. New York: Harper Perennial, 1991.

—. *Their Eyes Were Watching God.* New York: Harper Perennial Classics, 2006.

Irigaray, Luce. *The Sex Which is not One.* Trans, Catherine Porter. New York: Cornell University Press, 1985.

Jackson, Chuck. "Waste and Whiteness: Zora Neale Hurston and the Politics of Eugenics." *African American Review* (2000): 639-660.

Jones, Sharon L. *Critical Companion to Zora Neale Hurston: A Literary Reference to Her Life and Work.* New York: Facts On File Incorporation, 2009.

Lund, Vanessa. "Metaphors in *Their Eyes Were Watching God.*" 4 Nov. 2012. <https://sites.google.com/site/studytewwg/metaphors-in-their-eyes-were-watching-god- by-vanessa-lund-1>

Kaplan, Carla. *The Erotics of Talk; Women's Writings and Feminist Paradigms.* New York: Oxford University press, 1996.

---.*Zora Neale Hurston; A Life in Letters.* New York: First Anchor Books Edition, 2003.

King, Lovalerie. *The Cambridge Introduction to Zora Neale Hurston.* Cambridge: Cambridge University Press, 2008.

Kubitschek, Missy Dehn. ""Tuh De Horizon And Back": The Female Quest In *TheirEyes Were Watching God.*" *Black American Literature Forum* 29.2 (Autumn, 1983): 109-115.

Lee, Yu-fen. "Janie's Journey: Language, body, and Desire in Zora Neale Hurston's *Their Eyes Were Watching God.* Thesis. The National Sun Yat-sen University, 2007.

Longman Advanced American Dictionary. ed, New. Essex: Pearson & Longman, 2007.

Lyle, Timothy. "Zora Neale Hurston as an Independent Woman: A Lonley Place in the Harlem Renaissance." 27 April 2012. <www.timothylyle.com/.../Zora%20Neale%20Hurston>.

McGlamery, Tom. *Protest and the Body in Melville, Dos Passos, and Hurston*. Ed. William E. Cain. New York: Routledge, 2004.

Melo-Thaiss, Janet. *"Viva L'Orange*: Writing in the Open and Outlawed Space of a Feminine Economy." *Third Space: a Journal of Feminist Theory & Culture.5.2.* (Winter 2006). 2. Nov. 2012. <http://www.thirdspace.ca/journal/article/viewArticle/melo-thaiss/134#>

Moi, Toril. *Sexual/Textual Politics*. New York: Routledge, 2006.

Porter, A.P. *Jump at the Sun; The Story of Zora Neale Hurston*. Minneapolis: Lerner Publishing Group, Inc., 1992.

"Quizzez." *Novels for Students.*Vol.3. Gale Cengage, eNotes.com. 2, Nov,2012 <http://www.enotes.com/Theri-eyes/>

Richter, David E. *The Critical Tradition; Classic Texts and Contemporary Trends*. Fourth Edition. New York: Bedford/St Martin's,1997.

Sarup, Madan. *An Introductory Guide to Modernism and Postmodernism*. Hertfordshire: Harvester Wheatsheaf, 1993.

Saturday Review. "Books." 4. Jul. 2012. < http://zoranealehurston.com/books/seraph-on-the-Suwanee>

Selden, Raman and Peter Widdowson.*A Reader's Guide to Contemporary Literary Theory*. Hertfordshire: Harvester Wheatsheaf, 1993.

Sellers, Susan, ed. The Hélène Cixous Reader. London: Routledge, 1994.

Smith, Zadie. *Changing My Mind; Occasional Essays*. New York: The Penguin Press, 2009.

Sokhanvar, Jalal. *The Practice of Literary Terminology*. E.D. Maryam Beyad & The Editorial Staff of SAMT. Tehran: SAMT, 2001.

Tate, Claudia. "Hitting "A Straight Lick with a Crooked Stick": Seraph on the Suwanee, Zore Neale Hurston's Whiteface Novel."In Harold Bloom, *Zora Neale Hurston*. New York: Infobase Publishing.

Tyson, Lois. *Critical Theory Today: A User-Friendly Guide*. 2nd Edition. New York: Routledge, 2006.

Walker, Alice, ed. *I Love Myself When I Am Laughing and Then Again When I Am Looking Mean And Impressive*. New York: The Feminist Press, 1979.

Walker, Alice. "Zora Neale Hurston." 4. Jul. 2012. <http://zoranealehurston.com/>

Wolfgram, Teresa. *"Their Eyes Were Watching God."* 2. Nov. 2012. http://tewwg-l itwebpage.blogspot.com/2009/12/literary-device-evaluation_13.html

| نام واحد دانشگاهی :تهران مرکزی | کد شناسائی پایان نامه :1012031902004 |

عنوان پایان نامه :بررسی "چشمهایشان رو به خدا بود" و "ملک مقرب بر فراز رود سوانی" از خانم زورا نیل هارستون" در منظر هلن سیکسو

| نام ونام خانوادگی دانشجو: ایران زمانی سیبینی | تاریخ شروع پایان نامه :بهمن 89 |
| شماره دانشجوئی : 86080527٠ | تاریخ اتمام پایان نامه :آذر 91 |

استاد/ استادان راهنما :دکتر نجومیان

استاد/ استادان مشاور:دکتر آرین

آدرس و شماره تلفن :قزوین- محمدیه- منطقه 5 – سرو 47 پلاک 25- 09390935652

چکیده پایان نامه:

زورا نیل هارستون از چهره های خوش نام در عرصه های ادبیات آفریقایی –آمریکایی و مطالعات زنان است. پژوهشگر بر آن است که خوانش شاهکار وی با عنوان "چشم هایشان رو به خدا بود" به همراه اثر داستانی دیگرش "ملک مقرب بر فراز رود سوانی" را از منظر تئوری های منتقد و متفکر فمینیست پساساختارگرای فرانسوی مورد خوانش قرار دهد. رمان های منتخب دارای ویژگی های برجسته ای می باشند که پژوهشگر را بر آن داشته اند تا آنها را را از دیدگاه سیکزو مورد بررسی قرار دهد.هدف اساسی این پژوهش، بررسی دقیق این است که آیا رمان های انتخاب شده می توانند نمونه هایی از مدل نوشتاری زنانه تلقی شوند.اولین ویژگی قابل ملاحظه وشایسته توجه این است که این رمان ها حاصل نگارش یک بانو می باشند. دومین ویژگی قابل ملاحظه در هر دو داستان، وجود قهرمانان زنی است که در مقابل الگوهای پدرسالاری طغیان می کنند.با مطالعه ی مفهوم های محوری پویایی، تکثرگرایی، کالبد که گونه ای از پایداری در مقابل ساختارهای پدرسالارانه است و غلبه ی صدا که یک عنصر واژگون کننده در متن می باشد،این پایان نامه به این نتیجه می رسد که: "چشم هایشان رو به خدا بود" و "ملک مقرب بر فراز رود سوانی" می توانند ویژگی های پساساختارگرایانه و همچنین الگوهای زنانه را در خود جای دهند. به بیان دیگر، زورا نیل هارستون، نویسنده ی این رمان ها می تواند به عنوان یکی از الگوهای سیکزویی نوشتار زنانه تلقی شود.

کلمات کلیدی : نوشتار زنانه – پساساختارگرایی – پویایی – تکثرگرایی - صدا

نظر استاد راهنما برای چاپ در پژوهش نامه دانشگاه   مناسب است   ☐

مناسب نیست   ☐

تاریخ و امضاء

تشکر و قدردانی:

سپاس بی پایان پروردگار بی همتا را که مرا در تمامی مراحل زندگی ام از جمله علم اندوزی و هم چنان به ثمر رساندن این پژوهش یاری نمود و هیچ گاه مرا از لطف بی منتهایش محروم نساخت. پس از آن مراتب تشکر و سپاسگزاری فراوان خویش را از صمیم قلب خدمت استاد راهنمای بسیار گرانقدر، دانشمند و دلسوز خویش جناب آقای دکتر امیرعلی نجومیان که با شکیبایی تمام بنده را امر نگارش این پایان نامه یاری نمودند به جای می آورم. هم چنین از سرکار خانم دکتر آزیتا آرین، استاد مشاور بسیار فرزانه که با دقت و حوصله در تهیه این پژوهش یاری ام رساندند بی نهایت سپاسگزاری می نمایم. با سپاس، تقدیر و تشکر فراوان خدمت مدیریت محترم گروه تحصیلات تکمیلی دانشگاه آزاد اسلامی واحد تهران مرکزی، جناب آقای پروفسور جلال سخنور به پاس تمامی زحمات بی دریغ و راهنماییهای با ارزشی که ایشان نه تنها در مقام مدیریت محترم گروه بلکه در مقام استاد داور به اینجانب ارزانی داشتند.

سپاس بی پایان اما ناچیز خویش را خدمت تمامی خانواده ام و به خصوص پدر و مادر بسیار عزیزم سیاوش و عالیه زمانی و همسر دلسوز و صبورم ایوب پاکذات و سایر بستگان و دوستانی که به نوعی به همراه من درگیر انجام این پژوهش بوده و مرا در تمامی مراحل پر فراز و نشیب تکمیل آن یاری رساندند، تقدیم می نمایم.

در پایان، وظیفه خود می دانم که از کارمندان گرامی اداره محترم پژوهش، آموزش و سایر پرسنل محترم دانشگاه آزاد اسلامی واحد تهران مرکزی که به اینجانب و سایر دانشجویان در این مسیر دشوار تهیه و تدوین پایان نامه یاری می رسانند تشکر و قدردانی نمایم.

تقدیم به :

پدر و مادر بسیار دلسوز و زحمتکشم :

سیاوش و عالیه زمانی سیبنی

و همه آنهایی که در آستانه اند.

به نام خدا

منشور اخلاق پژوهش

بایدی از خداوند سبحان و اعتقاد به این که عالم محضر خداست و همواره ناظر بر اعمال انسان و به منظور پاس داشت مقام بلند دانش و پژوهش و نظر به اهمیت جایگاه دانشگاه در اعتلای فرهنگ و تمدن بشری ما دانشجویان و اعضاء هیات علمی واحدهای دانشگاه آزاد اسلامی متعهدی کردیم زیر را به هنگام فعالیت های پژوهشی مد نظر قرار داده و از آن تخلی کنیم:

۱-۱ اصل برائت: التزام به برائت جویی از هرگونه رفتار غیر حرفه ای و اعلام موضع نسبت به کسانی که در حوزه علم و پژوهش را به رفتارهای غیر علمی می آلایند.

۲-۱ اصل رعایت انصاف و امانت: تعهد به اجتناب از هرگونه جانب داری غیر علمی و حفاظت از اموال، تجهیزات و منابع در اختیار.

۳-۱ اصل نروری: تعهد به روایج دانش و اشاعه نتایج تحقیقات و انتقال آن به همکاران علمی و دانشجویان به غیر از مواردی که منع قانونی دارد.

۴-۱ اصل احترام: تعهد به رعایت حریم و حرمت ها در انجام تحقیقات و رعایت جانب نقد و خودداری از هرگونه حرمت شکنی.

۵-۱ اصل رعایت حقوق: التزام به رعایت کامل حقوق پژوهشگران و پژوهیدگان (انسان، حیوان و نبات) و سایر صاحبان حق.

۶-۱ اصل رازداری: تعهد به صیانت از اسرار و اطلاعات محرمانه افراد، سازمان ها و کشور و کلیه افراد و نهادهای مرتبط با تحقیق.

۷-۱ اصل حقیقت جویی: تلاش در راستای پی جویی حقیقت و وفاداری به آن و دوری از هرگونه پنهان سازی حقیقت.

۸-۱ اصل مالکیت های مادی و معنوی: تعهد به رعایت کامل حقوق مادی و معنوی دانشگاه و کلیه همکاران پژوهش.

۹-۱ اصل منافع ملی: تعهد به رعایت مصالح ملی و در نظر داشتن پیشبرد و توسعه کشور در کلیه مراحل پژوهش.

دانشگاه آزاد اسلامی

واحد تهران مرکزی
دانشکده زبانهای خارجی،
گروه زبان و ادبیات انگلیسی

پایان نامه برای دریافت درجه کارشناسی ارشد (M.A)
گرایش : ادبیات انگلیسی

عنوان :
بررسی رمان های "چشم هایشان رو به خدا بود" و
"ملک مقرب بر فراز رود سوانی" از زورا نیل
هارستون در منظر هلن سیکسو

استاد راهنما :
دکتر امیرعلی نجومیان

استاد مشاور:
دکتر آزیتا آرین

پژوهشگر:
ایران زمانی سیبنی
آذر 1391

CPSIA information can be obtained
at www.ICGtesting.com
Printed in the USA
BVHW031640080321
601998BV00007B/709

9 783656 943518